Praise

'Deeply compassionate, profoundly inspiring.
A powerful call for STEM women to align their
careers for fulfilment with personal integrity.
These pages speak to the power of reclaiming
the intentionality of where to focus your time
and attention.'

— **Nir Eyal**, former Stanford lecturer,
behavioural design expert, and
international bestselling author of
*Indistractible: How to control your attention
and choose your life*

'Want to break free from the confines of conventional
careers and step into a world of intentional
success? Let *Intentional Careers for STEM Women* be
your guiding light. Get ready to transform your
professional life and unleash your full potential. But
it doesn't stop there. This book is a rallying call for
diversity, equity, and inclusion in leadership. It is
time for women with STEM backgrounds to step into
positions of influence and power – and shape a better
future for all.'

— **Lily Satterthwaite**, Regional Lead,
Microsoft, and Co-Lead, Global Technical
Women Committee

'I wish I'd had access to this book when I was earlier in my STEM career. It's educational and inspiring, providing tangible advice and proven methodologies. Don't hesitate to read this. You'll discover ways to empower yourself and create the fulfilling STEM career you deserve, while enjoying the journey along the way.'
— **Professor Alexandra Knight CEng FIMechE FWES**, founder and CEO, STEMAZING

'A gem of a book for STEM women about the power they have not only to navigate, but to purposefully, courageously, and authentically design rewarding, fulfilling, and highly successful careers. It's a must-read, crammed full of tools, techniques, and tips which, if actively implemented, will be game changers.'
— **Francesca Long**, Head of Training and Talent Development, The Faraday Institution

'If you know something isn't working for you in your current role then this book is for you. It will give you the tools and actions to put you in the driving seat of your career, enabling you to make career moves that align to your values and natural talents.'
— **Dr Helen Niblock**, Head of Regional Engagement North East, Yorkshire and Humber, EPSRC

'In the confusing world of STEM careers, this book is a guiding light that all women can look to. The stories that Hannah shares in this book are so relatable, and her inspiring insights can help women realign their career trajectories and empower them to reach their full potential.'
 — **Beth Clarke**, award-winning software engineer and STEM advocate

'This is the book I wish I'd had walking into the workplace as a woman in STEM. I'm so grateful to have the opportunity to implement these tools and techniques today. I will refer back to this book over and over again as I purposefully design my future career.'
 — **Marie Hemingway**, award-winning founder and CTO, Speak Out Revolution

'A must-read for every STEM woman, regardless of the stage she's at in her career. This book contains everything a great sponsor and mentor should tell you. It's a one-stop shop for all the internal and external work every woman needs to do to shine in her profession, to be her authentic, wonderful self, and to have a career that reflects this beauty.'
 — **Sadia Salam**, Executive Coach and Inclusion Facilitator, Sadia Salam Coaching

HANNAH ROBERTS, PhD

INTENTIONAL CAREERS *for* STEM WOMEN

SIX STRATEGIC STEPS TO BALANCE, CONFIDENCE AND FULFILMENT

R^ethink

*I dedicate this book to the people who harness
their unique talents to improve the world.
May the insights within empower you to
create a world that works for everyone.*

Contents

Foreword

Want to break free from the confines of conventional careers and step into a world of intentional success? *Intentional Careers for STEM Women* is your ticket to redefining what it means to thrive in your professional life. It is a powerful call to action for women with STEM backgrounds to take control of their professional lives, embrace their unique strengths, and create careers that truly fulfil them.

This book challenges the norms and offers a fresh perspective on career development. It is not just for women in STEM; its principles resonate with anyone seeking a more intentional and purposeful path. Hannah Roberts acknowledges that gender is a spectrum and extends a warm welcome to all who identify with the book's message. This book is beyond doubt a guide for anyone seeking a purpose-driven career.

Embracing inclusivity, it invites all readers to discover their true potential and make a lasting impact.

At its heart is the Career Pivots® Compass methodology: a transformative framework that guides us through six strategic steps towards balance, confidence, and fulfilment, equipping us with practical tools and actionable advice. What sets this book apart are the real-life case studies and client transcripts that vividly illustrate the principles and practices discussed. These stories provide valuable context and inspiration, allowing us to witness the transformative power of Hannah's approach. By sharing the experiences of her clients, she demonstrates that intentional career development is not an abstract concept, but a tangible and achievable reality for anyone willing to embrace it.

It doesn't stop there, though. This book is a rallying call for diversity, equity, and inclusion in leadership. It is time for women with STEM backgrounds to step into positions of influence and power and shape a better future for all. Hannah's commitment to achieve this is palpable.

In 2022, I was searching for a speaker on imposter syndrome for our new Unleash Your Power joint initiative between Microsoft and HSBC, and I was introduced to Hannah by the founder and CEO of Speak Out Revolution, Frances Holmes. She told me that Hannah has a unique take on imposter syndrome – and she wasn't wrong! After she delivered a 90-minute workshop as a pilot, the feedback was unanimous, and I extended the invitation for Hannah to speak at Microsoft's headquarters for International Women's Day. Since then, I have been championing and supporting her mission, because when every voice is heard, and every contribution is valued, we will have solutions fit for all members of society.

As you embark on this journey of self-discovery and intentional career development, remember that the path may not always be easy. It requires courage, self-reflection, and a willingness to challenge societal expectations. Yet the rewards are immeasurable: finding fulfilment, making a meaningful impact, and living a life that is aligned with your values and aspirations.

Are you ready to break free from the ordinary and create a career that truly matters? Then let *Intentional Careers for STEM Women* be your guiding light. Prepare to transform your professional life and unleash your full potential. Embrace the journey, unlock your potential, and make your mark on the world. Your intentional career awaits. Are you ready?

Lily Satterthwaite,
Regional Lead, Microsoft, and
Co-Lead, Global Technical Women Committee

Introduction

The idea behind a conscious career is being intentional about our choices and actions. Stepping onto a career conveyor belt that has a clearly defined pathway ahead, and striving to reach the top, does not result in success or happiness for the majority of professionals on that track. Those who stay and don't progress feel like failures, and those who leave feel they have failed by default. It's time to reinvent how we approach our careers, with a methodology that encompasses all aspects of our lives, so that we can fulfil our full potential.

This book has been written specifically for women with a STEM (science, technology, engineering or mathematics) background, particularly those in the first fifteen years of their career post-PhD. If you have picked up this book and work outside this sector, the methodology will still be relevant to you, but the examples and client stories may not chime in the same way with your experiences. I am also conscious that I have expressly used the word 'women' to define my readers. Gender is a spectrum of biological, mental and emotional traits. My definition of a woman is anyone who identifies as a woman at any point along that continuum. If you have picked up this book because its content resonates with you, then you belong and are most welcome here. There is something to learn no matter how you identify in terms of gender.

Whether you are working in the academic field or have moved beyond academia, there are a few key elements that bind women with a STEM background together. It is likely that you're constantly proving yourself, which means you end up working way beyond your contractual hours. Even at home your mind is still at work, and not fully present for the people and things that mean most to you.

In many cases, you are then overlooked, underappreciated and underpaid for all that hard work. Resentment creeps in and the longer you spend feeling paralysed by not knowing what to do next in your career, the less confident you feel.

Getting easily destabilised by specific people or even an email results in anticipation anxiety, overthinking and ruminating to the point of catastrophe, which drives that cycle of overworking to compensate for how you feel about yourself. If you have more than twenty-five years left in your career, this is unsustainable. I get it. Oh, how well I know all those challenges.

It turns out that, contrary to my belief when I was experiencing the scenario outlined above, I was not alone in feeling that way. Data-driven insights from thousands of my clients and spanning six continents reveal the same three major issues: unsustainable working practices, eroded confidence and feeling undervalued. I want you to know it doesn't have to be that way; things can be different.

In 2010, I was a pregnant postdoc on a twelve-month contract. The pressure to prove myself in the new role, and have a job to come back to after maternity leave, caused me to work way beyond healthy limits. I had zero boundaries and, what's more, I felt like I had no choice. No one outside of academia understood why I cared so much. I turned into Superwoman just to survive.

I was continually asking myself the question 'What's next?', but I didn't create the time or space to think about the answer. If I'm honest, I wouldn't have known where to begin. Instead, I unconsciously allowed my career to unfold in front of me. After taking opportunities presented to me, I became disconnected from my goal of trying to make a difference. I told myself to stay put and keep the stability and flexible part-time working pattern until my family was complete. This was a challenge because I had pushed my scientific project manager role far beyond its original parameters. Being the managing director of a spin-out company was definitely not in my job description.

On my third and final maternity leave, I knew something had to change. *I* had to change. Eight weeks into that maternity leave, my dad had a huge heart attack. It left me asking myself the big questions. What would happen if I died today? What tangible difference have I made in the world? That was the moment of realising I needed to do work that mattered to me, to see and feel the difference I was making every day, to feel fulfilled.

I embarked on a life-changing journey to restore my eroded confidence, learn how to prioritise my time and energy, and create a purposeful career. This book contains everything I learned, implemented and refined. It is the guide I wish had been beside me. I am now a professionally certified coach and trainer and, as founder of Intentional Careers™,[1] I'm on a mission to guide others to figure out 'what's next?' in their careers, and the strategy to make it happen, while balancing the things and people that mean most to them.

How this book can help

Have you ever had the experience of someone starting in your organisation after you and then leapfrogging ahead of you? They are the people who have a clear vision of what they want to achieve and where they are heading. They don't just work *in* their careers, they are constantly working *on* them too. They can articulate what they need and enlist the support of others in the process. If you recognise this person, rather than feeling resentful, it's time to create your own opportunities in a way that feels authentic to you. *Intentional*

Careers for STEM Women will be your complete guide. I'm going to give you a six-step methodology that will help you fast-track your way to being intentional in your career and elevate your balance, confidence and sense of fulfilment.

When you have a meaningful purpose, you make the shift from feeling tired all the time to feeling energised by your mission in the world. Laying the foundations of time and energy management ensures that you can make an impact without suffering from burnout. Overcoming personal limitations allows you to be comfortable and confident in your skin, giving you the freedom to add your unique value unhindered. You become highly sought after and better paid as a result. Finally, being conscious in your career design means learning to be a career architect: defining the navigational pieces alongside developing the skill set and mindset to implement your plan.

We live at a unique point in history when we are tackling some of the biggest questions facing the planet. We need more diversity, equity and inclusion (DEI) in leadership across all sectors. It is my hope that when an equitable and safe space is created for diverse leadership to flourish, the outcome will be solutions which are fit for not just a subsection, but all members of society. You may not feel like you have the capability or capacity to lead powerfully right now, but I see your potential, and you are remarkable.

You can't make good career decisions when you are overwhelmed, resentful or not feeling good enough.

That's why I advocate making the current situation as good as it can be, while simultaneously overcoming the thoughts, beliefs and behaviours that keep you small, and defining and taking microsteps towards what you want every week.

In *Intentional Careers for STEM Women*, I will guide you through the Career Pivots® Compass methodology.[2] You can take it slowly and gently or adopt the pace of an Olympic athlete – whatever works for you. However you decide to travel, you will be progressing through six strategic steps to balance, confidence and fulfilment, using the Career Pivots Compass framework: time and energy management, overcoming limitations, leadership pathways, career pivots, professional positioning, and propelling strategies.

Don't stop once you have completed all six steps. Every time you make a career pivot, explore it a little. Determine how much it aligns you with your goals, and recalibrate your vision to reveal your next step. Your levels of fulfilment will be supercharged with each pivot, so keep *Intentional Careers for STEM Women* with you every step of the way.

The principles of this book have been tested in over a dozen countries by over 1,000 STEM women, and they have proven to be universal. Woven throughout this framework are powerful insights from interdisciplinary research and thought leaders, and most importantly, client stories and transcripts from sessions with clients whose experiences and breakthroughs will help illustrate the principles and clarify your thinking. All clients have given their permission to have their coaching journey shared; however, some client names have been altered to protect their identities.

To show you how it all feels from the inside, I'll also share some examples from my own lifelong grapple with learning how to take off the protective armour of pushing, pleasing, perfecting, and making up catastrophe stories. I'll show you the pathway to finding inner confidence and direction. *Intentional Careers for STEM Women* contains powerful ideas, and the chapters are set out in a particular order for a reason.

The book is also arranged in three parts. Part One is designed to help you break free from an unconscious career by confronting the reality of your situation and building a strong foundation from which to rise. Part Two addresses a new way to authentic confidence. This is a game changer, because if there's one thing that traps us, it's low self-esteem. Part Three walks you through all the steps to make the transition from career bystander to career architect – not just what to do but how to tangibly achieve it. At the end of each chapter, in the 'Implement this' sections, I'll give you some thought and implementation exercises to make your journey as quick and easy as possible.

A journal will be a useful companion throughout this book, and especially for these exercises. Journaling is one of the most profound ways of engaging with your subconscious and allows you to tap into flow states, helping you to process emotions, harness creativity and keep track of events and moments.

I recommend getting yourself a lovely new note-book to accompany you on this journey. Who can resist stationery shopping? Equally, a pen and paper will suffice. You can type your notes; however, I have found that there is a deeper intuitive connection between your brain and hand, as opposed to between your brain and the keyboard.

Write your answers to the questions posed in this book, allowing whatever wants to flow out of your pen onto the page. It may be in written form, or sometimes it may be pictures and doodles. When writing, always ask yourself 'What else?' or 'What's underneath that?' It will make sure you don't skip over questions. Do not censor or judge your writing. If one journaling session turns into a to-do list, or moaning, just allow it. Dump it all out, and then get back to the real questions at hand.

You may find yourself resisting journaling or skip-ping the questions at the end of each chapter. You may tell yourself other things are more important. My only request, in the interest of you creating an intentional career, is that you give these sections a try.

It is not difficult to have an intentional career in the next six months if you take the steps outlined in this book in the order prescribed, and if you implement them to a high standard. You will hold up a mirror to yourself and that can feel challenging at times. Let me reassure you that all the things you are seeking are on the other side of partnering with your vulnerability. That's when the things that felt impossible become possible. You'll be living the life you want to be living. Deserving. Capable. Enough.

PART ONE
BREAKING FREE FROM UNCONSCIOUS CAREERS

In an unconscious career, as time progresses, you become less clear on, or motivated towards, the direction in which you are heading. You are more reliant on other people's opinions of what you should do, taking opportunities simply because they are offered, or even acting on pure serendipity. I'm not saying an unconscious career is necessarily a bad thing, just that there is another more aligned and conscious way.

We are living in a different world today than the one we were living in a decade ago. We are entering a new career era. In the past, we were taught to get a good education so that we could get a good job and save for retirement, when we would be able to enjoy ourselves and be happy. That was never going to be enough for millennials like me, and it certainly won't wash with Gen Z or Gen Alpha. Economies fluctuate according to the effects of major world events. We are digital and global, and above all we want purposeful work that makes a positive contribution to the world's biggest problems, while allowing us to balance the things and people that mean the most to us. Everything is at stake, and so our careers must reflect this.

1
Careers Fit For The Third Millennium

It was the first day of spring 2015 and I met up with an old friend at her house. While our kids were running around the garden, I asked her how work was going. As a patent law attorney, she had applied for at least six internal promotions in the previous three years, each one unsuccessful. She said, 'I tried so hard for so long to get a promotion and every time I've been overlooked. So, I've decided to just stop caring about work. I'll show up and do what's required of me, no more, no less. I won't be taking on extra projects or staying late.'

She was 'quietly quitting' – a term coined by @zkchillin (now @zaidleppelin) on TikTok in 2022 that proved so catchy and resonated so deeply the video that introduced it went viral.[1] Quietly quitting isn't about setting boundaries: that's something we all need to do to make sure we maintain our health and relationships. No, quietly quitting, as organisational psychologist Adam Grant says, is what happens when leaders breach trust and employers violate the unwritten expectations for how employees should be treated.[2]

Colleagues who started at the same time as my friend, and others she had personally trained, had been promoted ahead of her. There was an expectation that of course she would be promoted too. Over time, every failed interview further broke down trust levels until she had reached this point: feeling stuck, not wanting to leave without having any clarity on 'what's next?', but feeling the pull of the secure monthly wage and flexible working pattern she had already negotiated, which made family life work.

After that conversation I reflected for a while. When I applied for a promotion, I was overlooked and discriminated against on the grounds the role involved travel and was therefore not suitable for someone with young children. I wondered what life would be like if I saw my career as just a job rather than something that consumed me. I was spending more hours a day working than sleeping or seeing my children. What I was doing had to mean something; otherwise, what was it all for? Money? No. Quietly quitting just wouldn't work for me. I needed a different way.

The grass is always greener – or is it?

A client of mine, Liz, a senior scientist in a large multinational pharmaceutical company, came to me faced with this exact dilemma. She had been in her position at work for four years, and had been promised a promotion a year previously, which had not materialised yet. Her manager relied heavily on one person, and that person was not her.

Resentment was building, to the point where Liz kept her mouth shut, her head down, and focused on getting the job done. Feeling demotivated and unfulfilled was uncharacteristic because she was usually buzzing with new ideas and unique perspectives. She cared deeply about the work and the impact it created. She wanted to step up and felt ready for a new challenge.

Then it happened. A new job opportunity appeared like a bright shining beacon of hope. A fresh start was just what she needed – or was it?

If you are trying to get away from the overbearing or absent boss, backstabbing colleagues, and the culture of evening and weekend working being seen as standard, simply changing jobs may not work because, unfortunately, whatever the situation is, it can play out in a different environment. Why? Because you take yourself and your approach to dealing with these situations with you wherever you go.

Rather than quietly quitting, I am a strong advocate for making the current situation as good as it can be by identifying the root cause of the challenges you are facing and developing a toolkit of resources to approach these situations differently. Do all this while defining what it is you want, and take microsteps towards that goal every day.

There's nothing lost by applying for the bright shiny object; just make sure first that it is something you want, rather than the great escape. This is the difference between having an intentional career you are moving towards as opposed to one you are trying desperately to get away from.

COVID-19 changed everything

The World Health Organization declared the COVID-19 outbreak a public health emergency of international concern on 30 January 2020 and a pandemic on 11 March 2020.[3] I'm sure you remember exactly where you were the moment you realised daily life was about to radically change.

Two weeks prior to lockdown, my family and I had boxed up our possessions and put them in storage. The moment you see all of your possessions boxed up, you visibly see what you value in life. I had an extraordinary number of books, which disproportionately took up over half the boxes. I'm curious: what would it be for you? We left with only what we needed, no more, no less, for the next six months. Meanwhile the whole roof of our house was taken off as the extension work began to make room for our expanding family.

Interestingly, I had been craving a slowing down and simplification of life. I even had our names down to rent a caravan to live in during the extension work in a beautiful woodland nearby. No internet connection meant we would all interact with each other, and nature, in a different way. I for one was excited about the potentiality of connecting as a family without the interference of technology. Oscar, my eldest, was less enthusiastic, not being able to comprehend life without Wi-Fi, having been born as a digital native Gen Alpha.

The caravan fell through, and we ended up renting, but in a twisted turn of fate, my wish was granted and I got to experience simplification, just not in the way I had anticipated.

During lockdown here in the UK there were reports of goats taking over empty Welsh streets,[4] pollution-free skies over London,[5] and just for a moment our fast-paced lives slowed down long enough to pause and reflect, to ask ourselves, 'Is the life I have been living the one I want to be living?' Think back to that time in your life: what needed to change? Did you make it happen?

The (not so) Great Resignation

Some people did take action. An analysis by Gallup in 2022 found that globally only 22% of employees were engaged at work, and 45% believed it was a good time to find a job. In the UK the figures are worse for engagement, with only 9% of employees actively engaged in their work; however, the UK fared slightly better with only 40% of employees thinking it was a good time to find a new job.[6]

According to a survey by LinkedIn, 74% of those questioned indicated that time spent at home either during lockdowns or through working remotely during the pandemic had caused them to rethink their current work situation.[7] And the US Department of Labor reported that 11.5 million workers quit their jobs during the months of April, May and June 2021.[8]

It's easy to believe COVID-19 caused 'the Great Resignation', a term coined in 2019 by Associate Professor of Management Anthony Klotz for the mass, voluntary exodus from the workforce.[9] Figures reported in the *Harvard Business Review* show the quitting trend began over a decade earlier, and the pandemic simply added accelerant fuel to the already burning fire.[10] Data from the Chartered Institute of Personnel and Development reveals that the UK was suffering from a 'Great Suppression' in the twelve months prior to April 2021, when levels of job-to-job moves rose to a high of 3.2%, not seen for over fifteen years.[11]

The pandemic also found, widened and accelerated existing cracks in the fabric of our societies. Econometric analysis by Accenture Research reported that the COVID-19 crisis may have added as many as fifty-one years to the time it will take to reach gender equity.[12] In 2021, the World Economic Forum estimated the time required is now forecast at 136 years.[13]

On top of that, being a working parent during the pandemic was tough. I remember being exhausted.

One evening I took my daily walk at sunset around, of all things, a running track. All I could do was shuffle my legs and move at the pace of a snail. A stunning display of bright pink with deep hues of orange and speckled red brought a moment of colour to the challenging backdrop of my life. I know I wasn't alone in my struggles. A survey led by the charity Pregnant Then Screwed found that 57% of working mums believed that managing childcare during COVID-19 damaged their career prospects.[14]

The numbers don't lie. Your career matters, you matter. Are you willing to step onto centre stage and be the leading lady in your life? No more being the sidekick. No more support roles. The lead. Start by showing some compassion for yourself. Be honest. How are you doing, really? Only when we claim our lives can we find the power to do something differently.

What are you working for?

How would you answer the question, 'What are you spending the most time on at work?' Would you reel off a series of projects, people and tasks, or talk about the volume of messages in your various inboxes?

What if we replaced the word 'time' with 'energy'? How would you answer the question then? Seeking approval or people-pleasing, procrastinating, looking for recognition, perfecting or worrying? Do any of these words ring true for you?

CLIENT STORY
Dr Luciana Bellora – built on a house of cards

Luciana had recently started a research fellowship, but despite successfully taking this next step on the academic pathway, she was unsure if it was the right career path for her. During our first coaching session she said to me, 'When something at work doesn't go to plan, why does it feel like I'm starting from scratch with my confidence?'

It all began with the concern she had been using the wrong instrument settings to collect data. She worried it was a big mistake, and not just this data set would be affected, but all previous papers would need to be retracted – a certain catastrophe. Despite having performed due diligence up until this point, she felt compelled to spend the rest of the day ringing the instrument suppliers, and checking over and over again.

I asked her, 'What is concerning you most about this situation?' Luciana said, 'Getting this wrong would mean falling a long way. Not just this paper but all previous papers, and the fellowship was based on the methodology. I could be wrong and lose everything.'

If you have ever built a house using playing cards, stacking them in V-shapes, you will know just how precarious the structure is. Luciana's house of cards was built on the fearful foundations of being wrong, fear of failure and worrying what people would think. Then it collapsed: 'If I am no good at work then who am I? I'm nothing without my work.'

She had spent the whole day, and an extraordinary amount of energy, seeking approval from external sources to prove her worries were unfounded. At the end of our work together, she had managed to separate her self-worth from successes and failures, giving back time and energy to progress with truly fulfilling projects.

Successes and failures are outcomes. They do not determine your self-worth.

Knowing when it's the wrong match

Luciana discovered through our work together that her current role was a good match for her, and finding self-worth was the key to balance, confidence and fulfilment; but that is rarely the case for the vast majority of people. How do you *know* when something is the wrong match for you?

Put simply, your body will betray you first. Whether it is full-blown burnout, Sunday-night syndrome and you can't sleep properly, the sinking feeling of impending doom after returning from holiday, feeling less than excited, itchy skin or some other bodily cue, your body will point to the truth of it.

CLIENT STORY
Dr Zohra Butt – fear less

In 2021, I was one of five commissioned coaches working with groups of ten postdocs as part of a pilot project funded by UK Research and Innovation called the Prosper Project. The aim of the project was to help postdocs

move beyond academia by unlocking their potential.[15]
One of the main reported benefits of the group coaching
sessions was that individuals no longer felt alone.

Rereading the incoming journal entries was telling. One
of the postdocs, Dr Zohra Butt, was a big coaching
sceptic. She said, 'I can't see how coaching is going to
help me, it seems like a complete waste of time.' In one
of the first group coaching calls, I used an excellent
technique from Dr Pippa Grange's book *Fear Less: How
to win at life without losing yourself* and asked Zohra
to describe an image of her fear.[16] She answered: 'I'm
driving a car along the motorway. I want to get off
at the next exit, but I can't see what the signs say,
so I don't know exactly which exit to take, and the
car keeps speeding up all by itself.' The meaning is
clear. 'What is the ultimate role of fear in that image?'
I enquired. She said, 'To keep me in the car.' We can
interpret this to mean, 'To keep me in academia.'

I guided her back into the image, and asked how she
could alter the movie to move through the fear, or
make it disappear entirely. She said, 'I'm driving along
and I can see an exit coming up, so I put my foot on the
brake to be able to read the signs. I take the second
exit because there's one of those blue-and-white
viewpoint symbols and I park up on a grassy area, put
the handbrake on, get out of the car and have a picnic.'

She reflected back to me, 'I get it. I'm in charge of my
own car. I won't let fear make my choices. In fact, what
I actually want to do is finish this postdoc early and
have a couple of months' sabbatical before starting a
new job beyond academia.' Interestingly, that's exactly
what she did before starting the next chapter of her
career as a medical science liaison at Pierre Fabre UK.

The six big millennial-driven shifts

Pew Research Center predicts that by 2025, 75% of the global workforce will be made up of millennials – those born between 1981 and 1996[17] – although this statistic has subsequently been debunked by Anita Lettink, who questioned the legitimacy of this data. She reports that in 2025 millennials will be the largest group at work, but they will never represent 75% of the workforce by themselves. They will also not reach 50% (with the exception of Africa), unless a considerable portion of other age groups decide not to work anymore. Under current economic and financial conditions, that seems unlikely.[18] What is clear from the data though, is that millennials are a societal force, the biggest generation in history, even bigger than the baby boomers – those born between 1946 and 1964.

Yet millennials will experience the highest rates of unemployment and underemployment, with 34% of millennial PhD holders underemployed versus 10% of those without a PhD.[19] Gallup has some stark statistics too: 55% of millennials are not engaged at work, 60% are open to a new job opportunity, and 21% changed jobs in the last year, which was three times higher than non-millennials.[20] Your levels of fulfilment, therefore, are critical to your levels of engagement at work.

The six big millennial-driven shifts are from:

- Your pay cheque to your purpose

- Your satisfaction to your development

- Your boss to your coach
- Your annual review to your ongoing conversations
- Your weaknesses to your strengths
- Your job to your life's work

People want from their careers what they got from religion, spirituality and community in the past: a sense of identity, meaning, purpose; the opportunity to contribute; and a sense of belonging. That's a huge set of expectations. We're talking about work that gives people purpose beyond a pay cheque. Individuals leave workplaces because they are overworked, overlooked, underappreciated and underpaid. They will leave somewhere they feel miserable, and they will also leave somewhere they feel good, for something more.

Hirschman's research model – exit, voice and loyalty – provides some additional choices to quietly quitting. It essentially states you can have two possible responses if you are feeling dissatisfied at work: either leave or voice your concerns as a proposal for change that, if integrated, increases your loyalty.[21]

I am not a big fan of the 'grit your teeth and bear it' approach or 'quietly quitting'. These are not states that help you tap into your full potential. Throughout the rest of *Intentional Careers for STEM Women*, I'll show you how to speak up and change your situation, using my VOICE™ methodology.[22] We'll also cover how to progress, internally or externally, in a strategic and intentional way by addressing underlying fear.

After all, the choice to become unstuck and move out of paralysis only becomes available to those that can identify and move through fear.

I want to acknowledge that choice is, by definition, a privilege that not all members of society have. This is one of the many reasons I have pledged to be a B1G1 Business for Good.[23] I donated 10% of profits in the first two years of business to 500 Women Scientists, directly supporting nine fellows on the Fellowship for the Future leadership development initiative for women of colour in STEM.[24] In 2022, I read *Thirst* by Scott Harrison and Lisa Sweetingham and have chosen to champion clean water solutions because 771 million people in the world are living without clean water, and access to clean water means better education, income and health, especially for women and children.[25] I pledged tickets to various workshops, and at the time of writing the sales have given 12,000 days' access to clean water. Making a contribution to society beyond the tangible impacts of my primary business is rewarding and another way to experience fulfilment.

Just at the time when people expect the most from work, the 2020s and 2030s are predicted to be highly disruptive, due to several trends coalescing at the same time. The first is the mass retirement of baby boomers. Over half of all the money in the economy is controlled by baby boomers,[26] and every year between now and 2027 more of them will retire.[27] A lot changes when a person turns seventy: from earning, saving and investing money to drawing down on investments.

This is the greatest shift in wealth in history, and governments will need to grapple with reduction in tax payments, pension deficits and global supply chain issues.

No doubt these trends will be depicted in the media with sensationalising, shocking headlines; fear-inducing reasons to stay static, or even feel like you are going backwards in a period of instability when the opposite is true. It is a momentous moment in history, rich with incredible opportunities for those who can see and create them.

Don't let fear, whether it be your own or fear borrowed from the media, be in the driving seat of your career. Develop excellence in the usual job-seeking skills, such as tailoring your CV, building a successful LinkedIn profile, and honing your interview techniques. I will give you my fabulous top tips on these. You should also pay attention to the strategy of career design.

No matter what anyone says, career pivots shift identities; they are emotionally charged, and must be done with the utmost integrity. Of the LinkedIn users who responded to my survey, 89% agreed that changing roles or jobs was an emotional journey as well as a practical one.[28] I would love to say it's time to strap fear into the back seat of your car, or kick it out altogether. The reality is more interesting than that. You will be partnering your fear with compassion, and acceptance allows it to move through you, bringing you back to powerful choice and resourceful actions.

IMPLEMENT THIS

Journal on the following questions:

- What image comes to mind when you think about the next steps in your career?
- What does that image mean to you?
- What is the role of fear in that image?
- How can you change the image to move through or eradicate the fear? What would happen if you did?

Recognise that your current role, even if it is not fulfilling, is serving you in some way. What does it give you? This answer will be different for everybody, but here are some ideas to kick-start your thinking:

- Flexibility in working hours
- Flexibility in working environment
- Regular pay cheque
- Autonomy
- Nice co-workers
- You excel at it
- Safety

Make a note of what it is for you. When you get up tomorrow morning, say to yourself, 'This job gives me [insert your answer] and for that, I can be truly grateful.' In fact, say it to yourself every morning until you have implemented your next career pivot.

This is not toxic positivity. We are not going to put a sticking plaster over all the things your career is not and pretend they don't exist. This practice of being grateful for what is will go a long way towards managing those feelings of resentment while going through the Career Pivots Compass process.

2
Taking Ownership
Of Your Career

In this chapter I will take you through key moments in my personal journey. Although I reveal details about my unique path, I ask you to read it through your own life lens. Perhaps my words will be like a mirror, or an uncomfortable spotlight at times. When you extrapolate my experiences to your own life, you will gain the most insight. As you read, ask yourself the following questions:

- How does this apply to my own struggles?

- When have I felt similarly?

- How can I use the methodology in my own life choices?

- What questions did using the methodology raise?
- Where did it provide clarity?

This is where we do the deep work, so allow yourself to go into introspection and reflection mode. I know you are ready for this.

Like science? Be a scientist

The best way I know to help you understand your career is to take you back to the start. You may not realise this, but you probably actively stepped onto your career conveyor belt between the ages of four and ten. Your choice will have been based on personal passions, and parental or cultural expectations.

My unconscious career was passion-based. Growing up, I loved a book series called, *How My Body Works*.[1] Every other week there was a new book with a plastic lifelike body part stuck to the front of it and, over time, the parts built up into a 3D model of the human body.

I would look up into the night sky and write down what I observed, and I remember begging my mum and dad for a chemistry set for my birthday. My mum, in particular, was less than keen on the idea. She told me she had read in the newspaper that a child had made something from the chemistry kit which looked like orange juice, and left it by his bed. The child drank it in the night and died.

Not deterred in the slightest, I told her in no uncertain terms, 'I'm not stupid you know,' and agreed to strict control measures for the kit when not in use. The experiment I loved the most was using the methylated spirits Bunsen burner to heat up a test tube full of match ends until they were set on fire and a big plume of thick grey smoke snaked out of the top. In writing this now, I realise the huge privilege I grew up with.

I remember announcing to my parents at about the age of eight: 'When I grow up, I want to be a doctor.' I loved science and held a deep desire to heal people, and that was the only job I knew which had an expression of both. How about you? When did you first make an active choice about your career pathway? What did you want to be? What were the 'shoulds' or 'musts' from your parents or your culture influencing you?

'What do you want to be when you grow up?' is a question we ask a lot in our society. I've been to numerous preschool and school events where children were paraded out, each with a painting depicting their future self, and child after child would say, 'When I grow up, I want to be . . .' You'll always get some doctors, vets, train drivers, astronauts and footballers, but my personal favourites are the fairies and ninjas. When we focus on *being* something, that means there's some sort of final destination and we form an identity around it. Should we fall short and not achieve it, then it feels like failure.

Forming an identity around your career is not something I want to encourage in you, or future generations, because what you will discover in this book is that we will do almost anything to avoid feeling a failure.

Not quite good enough

The choice of eight-year-old me determined all the subjects I studied, from triple science GCSE to A-levels in biology, chemistry and mathematics. At A-level I liked the sound of new subjects like psychology and sociology, and I had a passion for art, but I was discouraged from taking these subjects and told to stick to the ones that were a requirement for medicine: your choices are biology, chemistry and maths, or biology, physics and maths. At this point, no one questioned my rationale for medicine; it was accepted as the only truth. We need to start asking where these decisions are being born. Looking back, what advice were you given that was potentially a barrier?

My dad took me to the medicine degree interview at The University of Manchester. As I was the first person in our family lineage to ever go to university, he couldn't advise on the process. We waited companionably in the car, and he gave me a few pages of *The Telegraph* to read. He was always cutting out interesting articles and saving them for me. Still does to this day.

I remember one of the interview questions clearly: 'You have been working on a group task with five other students. At the beginning everyone is pulling their weight, but one student starts to miss sessions and deadlines. What do you do?' I'm not going to tell you what I said, but the interviewers nodded with approval at my response and I got a place to study medicine. Hurray for eight-year-old me, job done.

The only slight problem was I missed the conditional offer by one grade. I rang the university and waited three days for them to tell me it was a no. For the first time in my life, I had failed at something that mattered, and with that disappointment in myself came some uncomfortable feelings. I couldn't separate out my self-worth from the outcome. I felt a sinking feeling deep inside my body. A hard knot in the left side of my stomach. The shameful feeling that I wasn't quite good enough.

The internal cracks of pressure

Instead of allowing myself to experience my feelings, reflect and move forwards, up came the emotional brick walls surrounding me, as I told myself I never wanted to feel like that again. Who can blame me, right? I'm sure you've had similar moments in your life, whether being dumped by your first love, caught by your parents with beer cans in the bin, or feeling desperately alone in a room full of people – sadly, all true for me. I also have a vivid memory of one of my brother's pivotal moments: his ashen face as he sat back against the wall of the house. We had arrived home to find the car wedged halfway through the fence.

With 'I'm not quite good enough' firmly imprinted in my system, I embarked on a chemistry degree, vowing to work even harder this time. I wouldn't make the same mistake again. Although this resulted in a first-class Master of Chemistry (MChem) and fourth position in the year, I was doing everything from the belief that I wasn't good enough to practise medicine. The cracks of this belief were starting to show as I held myself to ever-increasing internal standards and expectations. Like an amateur trying out the steeplechase, I wasn't sure if I could keep making the bar.

The first panic attack came in the final-year organic chemistry exam. I couldn't instantly get the answer to the first question, so my body went into panic mode and all I could think of was the percentage the exam was worth to my overall classification. I wanted to leave the room and run away to the toilets, but instead I was rooted to my chair just trying to breathe as my heart pummelled in my chest with rising panic. After what felt like forever, but was only a couple of minutes, I calmed down and decided to move on to the next question. Once my system had regulated itself, I whizzed through all the questions and found myself back at the start of the exam answering that dreaded question number one with no problem. I thought the panic attack was a one-off, but unfortunately it was only the beginning.

I did step off the academic career conveyor belt for a while, trying desperately to find my thing. One professor told me on the last day of term, 'You'll be back.' A bit like a cryptic reverse terminator statement, why was he saying this to me now? Maybe he had a magic eight ball on his desk, because I did come back to do my PhD four years later. In the meantime, I was accepted into the graduate development scheme at Croda Chemicals and worked for a couple of years before taking a maternity leave cover post as a research business manager in cancer studies at Cancer Research UK (formerly known as the Paterson Institute). I tried to reapply to university to study medicine; even then the pull to return to the original plan of my eight-year-old self was strong. In my final medicine interview, it was clear I wasn't going to be offered a place. They even told me I sounded like I wanted to research humans, not treat them.

Comparisonitis – where self-esteem goes to die

My self-esteem was at an all-time low. Everyone I knew was forging ahead and doing well in their careers, but not me. In my mind, I was continuously going back to the start line. How could someone with so much potential end up like this? Career error number 467 was doing a PGCE in secondary science. Don't let the distinction mark fool you; this was probably the worst professional experience of my life. I grappled with anxiety every time I had to teach a lesson and it increased to a crippling level. The worse lesson ever was bottom-set GCSE physics. I turned my back for one second and the students started pelting each other with colouring pencils. As the person in charge, I was shocked by their behaviour. I now feel a pang of guilt because when I was at school we used to steal magnesium strips, roll them up into a hole in the wooden desks, and set fire to them – but at least we waited for the teacher to leave the classroom first.

I battled with wanting to quit but not wanting the gap on my CV, and worried about what people would think if I didn't complete the course. It was obvious to me I couldn't continue to be a teacher, but I still had no idea what I wanted to be. The only solution I could find that I was happy with was to do a PhD while I worked on my mental health. Many of my clients report horror stories about PhDs that resulted in depression and anxiety. The supervisor lottery at its finest. I'm grateful it wasn't that way for me.

I treated my PhD as a nine-to-five job and rarely worked evenings or weekends. I started to feel pieces of me return. I embarked on my self-discovery journey with weekly counselling sessions. With three first-author papers and a total of nine overall from my PhD, you would think academic success from there was assured. This was not the case for me, and it may not have been the case for you either. There is a huge amount of luck in having an academic career that progresses beyond a postdoc. It requires insider knowledge of how the system works early on in your career, a system which is neither known nor obvious to first-generation university students. Not to mention the blockade of barriers for women and those from under-represented groups. If you are considering leaving academia or have already moved beyond it, you didn't fail. Your decisions bear no reflection on your talent.

You are talented. You are not your work. See your career as a pillar of your life rather than an identity to be proven.

The Intentional Careers journey

Instead of focusing on what to be in life, you can follow a series of predictable and repeatable steps to make the transition from leaving a career you unconsciously accepted to creating an intentional, purpose-driven career where you value yourself, feel valued by others, and make a valuable contribution to the world.

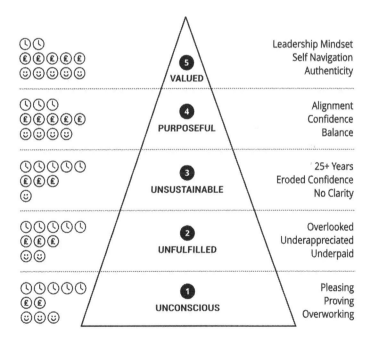

The Intentional Careers journey

Stage one is largely unconscious, the 'career conveyor belt' as I like to call it. This is where your career is viewed as a linear series of steps taking you to a final destination. In academia, that pathway is prescriptive: PhD, postdoc, fellow, lecturer, senior lecturer/reader, professor. No matter your industry, sector, function or area of expertise, there's usually a defined pathway to the top.

Did you actively step onto a career pathway, but then the rest of the process became largely unconscious as choices and opportunities presented themselves to you? The unconscious stage can last for not just years, but maybe even decades if you are not careful. It is the stage where you put the most time and energy into your work to please others and prove yourself. If you can just produce the most work, of the highest quality, surely the work will speak for itself, and you will be recognised and supported in your development by your manager as a result? Sadly, often this is not the case.

This is proving yourself at its finest, but where does it *really* get you? There seems to be an unwritten rule that when you start a new role or project, you must prove yourself for at least twelve months. This is one of the biggest barriers to career performance and trajectory.

During a proving cycle, you are actively seeking approval and therefore trying to claim your own self-worth in the form of external recognition from a manager or colleagues. Self-worth becomes wrapped up in how much you deliver. In a bid to please people, you end up saying yes to everything and making yourself the go-to person to get things done. That's when work becomes all-consuming, and work–life boundaries blur. Even when you are at home, your mind is switched on and busy.

It's as if you are a cup, and recognition and approval are the beverage of your choice. If your cup isn't full, you exercise specific behaviours to fill it up. The other problem might be holes in your cup. Those holes are your limiting beliefs about yourself, and your emotional allergies. We will talk more about these in Part Two. As someone is trying to fill your cup with approval and recognition, it's spilling out all over the place. We want to mend as many of the holes as we can and reduce the size of any holes we can't fix, so as much liquid stays in the cup as possible. If we also learn how to fill our own cup, we are no longer reliant on others. Our behaviours start to change, and any outsider additions are a welcome bonus.

Once a pattern of overworking is established, resentment creeps in and you start to feel overlooked, underappreciated and underpaid for all that hard work. Reliance on your manager for development starts to shift into thinking independently about the next steps, but clarity of direction is lacking. This is the moment when you think about asking for a pay rise, because if you were getting well paid for all the hard work you would feel better, right? Wrong. I'm not knocking a pay rise – it can certainly help – but does it really solve the underlying problem?

Stage two is the feeling of being unfulfilled, and will come with some identifiable, and unwanted, bodily manifestations. The problem is that you are living a paradox. The more you prove yourself, the further your self-worth depletes; you feel under-resourced in some way, and the insidious cycle continues. In a bid to deliver on all the things you have said yes to, you work harder. Health and relationships take a nosedive, and you end up feeling like you are failing in multiple areas of your life. Exhaustion and guilt set in, alongside a deep feeling of being undervalued for all that hard work. The lack of career clarity has you stuck, demotivated and disconnected from the impact of the role or organisation.

The longer you spend in the paralysis of stage two, the less confident you feel. Situations like this never remain static; they get worse over time. With over half of your career remaining, this way of working is unsustainable long-term. This is the moment to decide. Are you going to quietly quit, or are you going to say, 'No, that's not enough for me. I am valuable and deserve so much more than that'? I hope it is the latter. With the support of this book, it will be.

The motivation to change at **stage three** is so high it becomes compelling. Beware of the impulse to get away from your current situation, because this is not the moment to jump into whatever position's available, basing your decision solely on your skills and qualifications. It is well worth carving out the time to define what you want, and with that clarity, take confident action towards what is going to have you feeling purposeful, fulfilled and valued.

If you identify with being at stages one or two, the good news is you can skip straight to stages four and five, minimising unnecessary struggle. If you are at stage three, I'm sure you are already aware it's time to make changes.

All it takes is six strategic steps using my Career Pivots Compass methodology, which is outlined in the next section. You will learn how to make the shift from the unsustainable stage three to the purposeful **stage four**, where you will learn how to operate in alignment with your values, vision and natural talents. You'll rebuild your confidence levels and set strong work–life boundaries. By **stage five**, you will have mastered your leadership mindset, gathered your self-navigation tools and found a deep sense of authenticity. This will empower you to make your greatest contribution to the world.

One of my clients, research fellow Dr Noémie Hamilton, described the Intentional Careers journey beautifully. She said, 'At the start it felt like I was in a plane trying to land, but all I could do was circle around in the sky. Now I'm in control of my own plane. I've got the landing strip fully lit up and the ground staff waiting to support my descent and help me disembark. If this is the wrong airport, I've got more than enough fuel to fly back up and survey the next set of airports on my checklist, and I'll happily choose which one to fly to next and land there.' Buckle up because it's time to have your extended set of career pivot options highlighted in neon lights.

Fulfilment

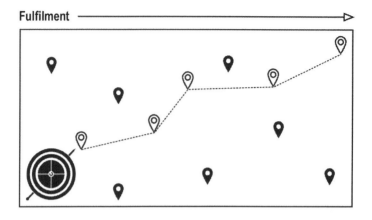

Glow in the dark

Introducing the Career Pivots Compass

After becoming a certified coach in 2018, I worked with thousands of clients on a one-to-one basis. Without fail, the three most sought-after outcomes were a better work–life balance, more confidence, and figuring out 'what's next?' in their career. All so they could make an impact and feel happy, be fulfilled and well paid for their efforts.

I noticed over time I had innovated a framework to help clients achieve these outcomes, which I now call the Career Pivots Compass. This methodology has allowed me to progress beyond one-to-one sessions and work with groups in my Career Design Mastermind™ programme,[2] at Intentional Careers events, and at scale through this book.

The Career Pivots Compass framework

You can't get the clarity you are looking for without carving out time in your schedule for personal and professional development. If you are too busy, head down producing, producing, producing, it's time to look up and work *on* your career, not just *in* it. That's why **step one**, a foundational layer of the Career Pivots Compass, is time and energy management: developing high-performance accountability habits to create the space for development while balancing the people and things that mean most to you.

Step two, the other foundational layer, is overcoming limitations. If you design a career from a position of eroded confidence, you are keeping yourself small. Work through my VOICE methodology to identify and overcome your personal limitations so you can create a career from the most well-resourced place possible. This will open a well of new potential that you didn't know existed within you.

Having secured the two foundational layers, we enter the inner part of the compass, where there are four remaining steps in the six-part strategy. The **third step** is to develop a leadership pathway based on your natural talents and strengths, and find mitigation strategies for your blind spots. This will help you to identify roles which are a perfect match for you and incorporate more joy, flow and excellence in your work. You will also identify how to flex your leadership and communication style, allowing you to work more effectively with, and through, other people.

Career pivots are the **fourth step**, which will help you to make the shift from proving yourself to adding value. This is achieved by connecting the 'dots' between your purpose, mission and vision, avoiding the capability trap, disconnected vision and values conflicts in the process, and gaining profound clarity on where to go next in your career. Each step is more fulfilling than the last, and every career pivot you make will move you closer and closer to the fullest expression of your purpose.

It shouldn't be this way, but in my experience a lot of job roles have been created with a specific person in mind. The advert is often tailored to that candidate's CV and experience, which makes it easy for the selection panel to say, 'Only this person fits the criteria, we have to hire them.' In an overcrowded job market, it has become even more essential to master the art of creating your own opportunities. That way you can become the person employers have in mind when writing their next job description. **Step five**, professional positioning, is a way to create your next career pivot using personal branding and online networking strategies.

It would be easy to assume the process is complete when you have a successful interview, but that couldn't be further from the truth. **Step six**, propelling strategies, helps you to capitalise on the transition by learning techniques to negotiate your salary, develop a 30-60-90-day transition plan to increase your chances of being promoted within the first two years, and gather feedback from your last role, alongside enhancing your natural talents to inform a new twelve-month personal and professional development plan.

In the coming chapters, I will take you step-by-step through each part of the framework to help you gain balance, confidence and a fulfilling career by being strategically intentional.

IMPLEMENT THIS

Reflect on your earliest thoughts about your career and jot down your answers to the following questions:

- When did you first make an active choice about your career pathway?
- What did you want to be?
- What were the 'shoulds' or 'musts' influencing you from your parents or your culture?
- Looking back, what career advice were you given that was potentially a barrier?

Review your current situation and assess which of the following stages of the Intentional Careers journey best describes it:

- Unconscious
- Unfulfilled
- Unsustainable
- Purposeful
- Valued

3
Foundations Of Time And Energy Management

From working with thousands of clients to generate their career values, I can tell you without fail that work–life balance almost always appears on the list. In an ideal world, balance comes from the policies, practices and culture a leadership team creates and sustains. In the absence or enforcement of these structures, agency and implementation are key to alleviating this form of dissatisfaction at work. In this chapter, I will support you in setting your boundaries and finding your voice.

Proving is passive; ownership is proactive. It all starts with using high-performance habits to find yourself one hour a week for personal development. It's time to move beyond the measure of how much you produce, and make the shift from time to energy management. Productivity does not equal success, recognition or promotional opportunities. Opportunities land in the laps of people who have clarity on what they want, can articulate what that is and enlist the support of others to help them achieve it.

You are the major asset in your career, not your laptop, you. If you go down, everyone and everything goes down around you. Start treating yourself like the major asset that you are. Remember: treating yourself like a precious object will make you strong.[1]

Pregnant? Career over

When I was in the final year of my PhD, I had just got married and my partner and I were thinking about starting a family. In a desperate search for a role model, I did some research and found that in a department of over two hundred, only five were women, and of those five, only two had young children. This left me wondering whether the academic pathway was even possible for me. I had conjured up an image of being a part-time professor and I couldn't find any real-life examples. Proof that representation does matter.

I thought my PhD was going to miraculously reveal to me what I wanted to do with my life, but instead, after four years I was none the wiser. After being recommended for a postdoc position, I took it. It's funny how I expected to gain career clarity, despite spending the total of zero minutes thinking about it.

Two weeks into that twelve-month position, I became pregnant and preoccupied with needing security and a contract to come back to after maternity leave. I became hypervigilant, because it always felt like there were hundreds of others waiting in the wings ready to take my place at a moment's notice. I said yes to everything and became the go-to person to get things done.

Just before I went on maternity leave, people offered up their advice, and I experienced a fair amount of nonconsensual belly touching. Clients have reported hearing out-of-touch, old-school viewpoints, such as, 'I got a nanny and returned to work after two weeks' and 'I wrote my fellowship in the first twelve weeks after giving birth.' Even more damaging is the recommendation to 'make maternity leave look like it never happened on your CV'. At the time, it may feel like people are just being helpful, but it comes at a cost. For me, that cost was feeling like I should be *doing* something with my maternity leave.

Five days after giving birth and having a one-litre haemorrhage, my face was streaked green and yellow under my eyes. It was horrific, and I had also temporarily lost the sensation of needing to wee. I may have had to stop every 100 metres to catch my breath, but that didn't stop me. I was back on my laptop, emailing the project partners from across Europe, putting together the impending scientific report for our funding body, Oscar fast asleep in his Moses basket next to my chair.

The rise of Superwoman

Needless to say, I wasn't one of those elusive women who could write a fellowship on maternity leave. I did try, but my heart wasn't in it. After staring at the blinking cursor, I closed the laptop and ended any notion of continuing an academic career. I never returned to the lab, gratefully clinging instead to the expanded scientific project management responsibilities that were offered to me on my return.

I continued to operate in that unsustainable way, spinning so many plates it felt impossible to put them down, convinced that everything would collapse around me if I did. Whenever I felt inadequate, incompetent or incapable, I simply flung more hours of work at the situation; but there are only so many hours in a day and there comes a point when that strategy starts to falter. That moment happened on my second maternity leave.

It was even worse than the first. This time I had two children under two, forming a tag team to wake me in the night, and all my work projects to manage. I was dizzy from exhaustion, and fielding important personnel phone calls in baby sensory classes. One time I had a boardroom full of men on speaker, all waiting for a strategic decision. I had the phone on hands-free while changing a stinker of a nappy to stop Oscar crying long enough for me to think of an answer.

How was everyone around me doing this? Were they thriving? I started to believe I was deficient in something. Maybe I was anaemic? I certainly looked it, but the blood tests revealed no problems. It turns out that I didn't have a deficiency in something, I had an excess of something, and that excess is what I like to call Superwoman. Running on fear and adrenaline, at top speed, to get things done.

What did I do next? What any other self-respecting Superwoman does. I took on another new project alongside my day job and started a spin-out company with three other female academics. My friend bought me a red 'superhuman' jumper in our Secret Santa draw at Christmas and I wore it with pride. I know what you are thinking: 'I want in on that Secret Santa.'

Do you know a Superwoman? Maybe you have been her in the past. Maybe you are performing your own version of her right now. Or do you yo-yo between being Superwoman and feeling anti-Superwoman? What impact are you having on yourself, and others, when you tell yourself, 'I have to do it; I have no choice. I'm exhausted and now I'm not productive enough'?

Little pea

Nothing changed until 2016. I was lying in bed one morning, scratching my armpits and discovering I hadn't shaved for a few weeks. Aside from the delightful image I'm conjuring up for you, I noticed a pea-sized lump in my left breast. Using my forefinger, I moved the little pea around, while my brain went from, 'It's nothing to worry about' to 'I'm going to die of cancer in around ten seconds.' Heart racing, adrenaline pumping, my cognitive function evaporated.

Two weeks later, I found myself alone, sitting outside the radiology department waiting room in a purple gown. After spending what felt like five minutes trying to find the little pea, and me telling the doctor 'I really do have a lump', they were able to mark it with a pen. X marks the spot. As I was waiting, another mum I knew from a mother and toddler class came down and sat next to me. I distracted her little boy, which seemed to ease her tension. It also helped calm my nerves. We exchanged numbers so we could check in with each other later.

As the radiographer ran the probe over the little pea, I was asked a strange question: 'Have you been very poorly recently?' 'No,' I replied. They said, 'You have a lymph node which has migrated from your armpit to your breast tissue. We usually see this in patients whose immune systems have been severely compromised. Are you sure you haven't been ill?' I shook my head in denial and was free to go, still unable to see the truth.

However, walking back to my car with relief washing over me, I had *my* moment of realisation. I had been going too hard for too long. Something had to change. I had to change. I had to be different. Perhaps you've had a moment of your own like that?

Five pillars of leadership

If you are expecting a great fanfare of recognition for sacrificing your health and relationships for work, be prepared for the fact that it may never come. If you are anything like I was and you have built your whole identity around your career, other areas of your life will be suffering. You will notice this particularly when you are under stress and feeling overwhelmed. What is the first thing to go when you feel under pressure at work? Is it your health? Do you stop exercising and eating well? Is it relationships? Do you work instead of spending time with the people that mean most to you? Are you working in your own head instead of being present in life?

To create a stable platform for your leadership and make your greatest contribution to the world, you need to build strong foundations by paying attention to five key pillars: health, wealth, relationships, career and personal development. Think of your pillars as the legs of a stool. Yes, I know, it's a weird five-legged stool. If, for example, you receive a life-changing health diagnosis, you are made redundant, your relationship breaks down or you need an unexpected house repair, this is the equivalent of a stool leg being kicked out. Having stability in the other pillar areas helps keep you upright overall. You can also think of your network as the sixth emergency pillar, stabilising you when you are challenged.

I invite you to complete a high-performance audit of your leadership pillars. Rate each pillar area out of 10, not as you would like it to be, but as things currently stand. A score of 10 out of 10 is: I'm doing amazing in this area and I can't see how it could be any better, whereas 0 out of 10 is: oops, I completely forgot that was even a thing in my life. Reflect on which pillar areas scored the lowest, and on where you would like to focus your attention for the next six months. This may or may not be the pillar with your lowest score.

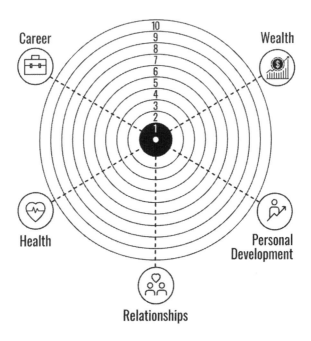

Performance audit

Now rate your energy levels today from 0 to 10. How many units of energy will it take to complete the work you have planned today? If it is more than the units available to you, then you can quickly see there is a problem. This is how energy deficits occur, which is fine for an isolated day but over time have a compounding effect that may lead to burnout.

A mentor once said to me, as I struggled even to find time to eat my lunch, 'If you can't take an hour for lunch because you are too busy, then you need to take three hours.' Let's dig into how we can put strategies in place to ensure you spend more time in energy abundance.

Destroying myself for what?

The Hybrid Ways of Working 2022 Global Report by Jabra shows that employees with full autonomy to choose where and when they work unanimously report a better work experience than those with limited or low autonomy.[2] Whenever I am speaking, coaching or training on the topic of getting control over your own time and energy, I am met with heated resistance. 'I can't even be fully present for this training, there have been twenty emails since we started thirty minutes ago,' stressed one participant. Believe me, I hear these concerns. In full-on Superwoman mode, I couldn't see an alternative either.

'It's only a few more days until the deadline,' I said to myself. I'd worked all day, done all the home stuff and there I was back with the computer screen glaring at me. It was nine in the evening and I felt dizzy, but still I pushed through to finish those colour-coded pivot tables before midnight.

One deadline quickly gets replaced by another, and another, and another. It is an insidious spiral that creeps up on you over time. I destroyed myself over several years for that job. When I left, I felt I was owed so much, and yet I was barely given an acknowledgement, just something along the lines of, 'Oh yeah, you really helped us out.' Helped you out? I destroyed myself for that job by deprioritising my relationships and my health.

If you are waiting for the validation, the acknowledgement, the praise, ask yourself what for. It may never come. You have to be able to validate and value yourself. To do this, you need to advocate for yourself in the workplace. Enforce your boundaries. Otherwise, you get what you have always got: no work–life balance. You need to work sustainably to make yourself the primary asset in your career. I understand barriers are real, and it may take different people different amounts of time and effort to find the safety to speak up and advocate for themselves. Societal obstacles may even need to be overcome in the process. As history has shown so far, this isn't necessarily going to be an easy fix. For example, the cost of courage for a person in a marginalised group is high because of the topics that need to be voiced, heard and overcome, such as speaking out against racism, protesting the killings of innocent minority people, and fighting for equity in a biased world.[3]

I was always looking for role models in the workplace. Analysing, assessing and deconstructing the people ahead of me; how they were working, behaving and responding. I tried my best to emulate them. With Superwoman as my armour, I did a good job of keeping up with them. An email at 10.29pm? Not a problem for me. I would respond immediately, as speed was imperative. The faster my pace, the more important and valuable as an employee I felt.

In the haze of my frenetic speed, I lost sight of the people coming up behind me. They were watching me too. Worst of all, emulating me. When a pregnant postdoc came to my office and said, 'What should I do about my return to work?', I felt disgusted with myself, so ashamed. I couldn't say, 'Do what I did.' For the first time, I wished I hadn't worked through those precious maternity leaves. I didn't want someone else to have the same experience as me. I wasn't a role model at all, and in that moment, I vowed to change.

The quote 'Be the change you want to see in the world' is often attributed to Mahatma Gandhi, but it is a paraphrase of his profound passage: 'We but mirror the world. All the tendencies present in the outer world are to be found in the world of our body. If we could change ourselves, the tendencies in the world would also change. As a man changes his own nature, so does the attitude of the world change towards him. This is the divine mystery supreme. A wonderful thing it is and the source of our happiness. We need not wait to see what others do.'[4]

You doing things differently paves the way for others to follow. Be the trailblazer you wish had been in front of you.

CLIENT STORY
Dr Yana Skliar – the weekend off

When I first met Yana, she was a research associate at a European research institute, and she hadn't had a weekend off in over four years. She not only wanted to clarify her career direction, but she also desired balance in her life. I distinctly remember the moment in our fourth session when she said that no one in her group could take holidays. If they asked, her manager would simply say, 'Well, how will you get everything done?'

We explored a structured, nonconfrontational conversation template to help her ask for what she needed, which at the time was a week's holiday. Following this structured approach, her manager had nowhere to go with the conversation, other than to approve her time off graciously – holidays that she is entitled to by law, I might add. Her colleagues saw that she had holidays approved, and they noticed an improvement in her confidence. She became their role model for setting boundaries, and this opened the gateway for them too.

On the back of this initial success, Yana reclaimed a month of full weekends, delegating parts of her experiments that had to be done in a seven-day sequence to competent colleagues. Likewise, once every six weeks she would repay the favour and do the same for them. The weekends off gave her time to enjoy her life outside of work. To visit art galleries and explore coffee shops with friends – some of the reasons she had been initially attracted to the city, beyond the job opportunity.

Rather than decrease her output, she experienced an increase in productivity, creativity and happiness. It was a real pleasure to witness her excitement and vitality returning.

When was the last time you did not work evenings or weekends? What has been the impact of overworking on yourself and others?

Finding the unicorn of work–life balance

By now you will be ready to do things differently. If you have prioritised your career over the other pillar areas in your life, it's time to start paying attention to all pillar areas because, as Nir Eyal, author of *Indistractible: How to control your attention and choose your life*, says, 'If you don't plan your day, someone or something else will.'[5]

If you come on this journey with me, you will be undertaking this process with your long-term vision plan, but for now, imagine where you would like to be in ninety days' time in each pillar area. To get to that target, what needs to happen? Do a big brain dump of everything and prioritise that list into A-, B- or C-level priorities. A is the highest-level priority for you, B is urgent things for other people, or less urgent and important things for yourself, and C is admin-type tasks, the kind where, once you get one done, there's always another to replace it – a bit like the hoovering in the house. Once in these categories, break down the tasks and sub-prioritise: A1, A2, A3, A4, etc. A task should be broken down into something which can be completed in a timeframe between forty-five and sixty minutes. Write your top priorities against each pillar for next week:

Pillar	A1 priority
Career	
Health	
Relationships	
Personality development	
Wealth	

If you struggle to find time for the pillar areas other than your career, my top tip is to put the activities for health, relationships, personal development and wealth into your calendar before any career tasks get scheduled. Otherwise, what tends to happen is the tasks allocated for anything other than career get ignored and eclipsed by work.

Go ahead and predict how long each of those tasks will take and block them into your calendar system right now. In particular, I'd love you to find one hour a week in your schedule for personal development, so that you can work *on* your career not just *in* it. By the time you get to the end of this book, you will be clear on your top-priority tasks to complete during these time blocks.

CLIENT STORY
Dr Rachel Dunmore – the productivity ninja

One of my clients, Rachel, a project manager in HR, blew me away with how proficient she became at implementing my time-and-energy-secrets strategies. On paper, Rachel has no control over her diary. Anyone can look at her calendar, book time with her and request she attends a meeting. She was at the behest of others' priorities and, as a result, often felt like she was firefighting and stretched too thinly.

After one of the Career Design Mastermind group coaching calls, she decided enough was enough, she was going to implement these strategies to their fullest. The first thing she did was speak to her manager about blocking out focus time for the mornings. Her manager said, 'Go ahead and try it for a week and then we can review how it's gone.' She was so productive her manager insisted it continued.

She didn't stop there. Next on her list was to change how she thought about meetings. She set up the calendar system to send an automatic reply saying she wasn't available during focus time: 9.30am–12pm. If her presence was required, the person had to email her with the request. As Rachel said when I interviewed her on my podcast, 'Half the time, meetings have no agenda and waste a lot of people's time. I am forcing people to rethink their attitudes towards meetings. Is my presence really needed or would the issue be best served with an email, an offline collaborative document or a different style of meeting?'

She is now referred to as 'ninja chair' at meetings because she doesn't waste a minute of people's time, and as we all know, time is one of the most precious commodities on earth.

 Listen to Rachel's full podcast episode at **https:// hannahnikeroberts.com/inspiring-stories-017-dr-rachel-dunmore**.

IMPLEMENT THIS

- Set weekly A1 priorities under each leadership pillar: health, wealth, relationships, personal development and career.
- Put all other pillar plans into your calendar first and career tasks last to prevent eclipsing everything for career.
- Set start and end of workday times as boundaries.
- Ensure there is at least one hour in your schedule every week for personal development.
- In your next personal development one-hour time block, complete the Intentional Careers Scorecard to determine which stage of the Intentional Careers journey you are at, and gain personalised insights to the most impactful steps you can take next. Visit: https://scorecard.intentional-careers. com/strategy.

PART TWO
A NEW WAY TO AUTHENTIC CONFIDENCE

There's a myth about confidence. You don't need more confidence to take action. It's the action-taking itself that breeds confidence, but even when you can find enough inner resources and courage to move forwards, it must be done in integrity with yourself. Those actions should come from your true authenticity.

I am sorry to break this to you, but there's no authenticity without vulnerability. Luckily, everything you are looking for is on the other side of meeting your vulnerability. It's time to stop running away from your feelings. Take a peek below the surface of your pushing, pleasing, perfecting and worrying to address the root cause of your lack of self-worth. That's when the magic will happen. An expansion into your true potential, your capabilities and fulfilment.

The investigation will be worth it. Treat yourself like an experiment. Try out the tools, keep what works for you and discard what doesn't. If there's something you are resisting, look closely at it. Usually, it will be the thing you need the most.

4
Imposter Syndrome

I was watching my daughter Elsie's swimming lesson and something strange was happening. The teacher would get all the swimmers to line up, but when Elsie got to the front, she was made to wait at the side, letting other swimmers continuously have turns without her. This went on for ten minutes of a twenty-five-minute lesson. I couldn't understand what was going on.

When I got to the poolside at the end to pick Elsie up, she ran at me, flung her arms tightly around my neck and cried. Like a cling-on koala bear, she did not want to ever let go, and was an inconsolable four-year-old for the rest of the evening. It turned out that when you don't listen properly at swimming, being displayed as naughty and missing out on the rest of the lesson is the punishment. A tactic to shame someone into conforming. The result? Elsie was adamant she would never go to swimming lessons again. Perhaps something similar happened to you in the past? An incident which had you take a defensive position, making you want to stop, avoid, hide or procrastinate. Maybe at school, at home, or even with friends.

It's moments like this, early on in our lives, that start a chain reaction inside us as we form emotional allergies: feelings we hate to feel and will do anything to avoid. Elsie felt so bad about herself, her way of controlling that feeling was to say, 'I never want to go to a swimming lesson ever again.' If she could avoid the situation, there would be no chance of feeling the feeling; a tactic that works to a degree, but seriously restricts our experience of life. I did this to myself for ten years with public speaking. I would do anything to get out of presenting and avoid the embarrassment of being shown up, and torn apart, for not knowing enough. The mental academic equivalent of being stripped bare in front of everyone.

This is what I said to her while stroking her head rhythmically: 'Sweetheart. Right now, you are feeling really sad and upset and I know it can be uncomfortable. It's important that you allow yourself to feel all of your feelings and allow them to move through your body.' After a while she stopped crying, and I told her, 'We don't make big decisions when we are feeling our feelings. We can make choices another day. So, what would make you feel good right now?' She said cuddles, Bun Bun (her super-soft white rabbit teddy) and the book, *Ten Minutes to Bed Little Unicorn*.[1]

It's the same way with our careers. When we try to make decisions about 'what's next?' from a position of eroded confidence, we are hindered by our insecurities. That's exactly why the second foundational layer of my Career Pivots Compass methodology is overcoming limitations. To fulfil our potential, we need to pull out the source of the problem at the root.

Three layers

When I first heard the term 'imposter syndrome', quite frankly I thought it was a load of bollocks. It was 2015, and a colleague came to my office raving about the revelations he'd had at an imposter syndrome workshop. I was super sceptical, but out of respect I asked him what it was about. He said giddily, 'You know, that feeling that you will be revealed to not know enough. That your boss will find out that you don't actually know what you're doing.' I felt so exposed by his synopsis, because I knew that sinking feeling of dread all too well. Maybe you do too?

The definition of imposter syndrome is, 'The persistent inability to believe that one's success is deserved or has been legitimately achieved as a result of one's own efforts or skills.'[2] The concept of imposter syndrome originated from Pauline Clance and Suzanne Imes's 1978 research paper 'The imposter phenomenon in high achieving women: Dynamics and therapeutic intervention', published in *Psychotherapy*, the journal of the American Psychological Association.[3]

For high-achieving, ambitious women, imposter syndrome is common. While statistics on prevalence vary wildly from 9% to 82% (depending on the screening tool and cut-off point used to assess symptoms),[4] a survey of more than 1,000 researchers suggests women in academia suffer from above-average levels of imposter syndrome. Participants were asked to take a Clance Impostor Phenomenon Score test, and the scores revealed 95% experienced moderate or intense levels of imposter syndrome.[5]

Over time, for some people, imposter syndrome can lead to working beyond sustainable efforts. Burnout was recognised by the World Health Organization in 2019 as an occupational phenomenon and included in the eleventh revision of the International Classification of Diseases.[6] According to the *Journal of BMC Psychology*, on average it takes six to eighteen months to recover from burnout.[7]

A quick back-of-the-envelope calculation for someone on a £40,000 salary, supported by UK statutory sickness pay during burnout recovery, would mean a reduction of 87% in salary,[8] plus long-term implications to their career trajectory. Getting stuck at around £40,000 per year without a promotion to up to £100,000 could mean losses of over £300,000 over five years and, assuming further promotional opportunities are lost, over £1 million over ten years. Huge ramifications not only for your long-term health, but also for your bank balance and financial legacy plans.

In 2018, I went to a conference led by Dr Joanna Martin, founder of One of Many™,[9] where she described the three main layers of imposter syndrome as: feeling any success is unearned or undeserved, over-crediting others, and using minimising language.[10]

Let's have a look at that first layer of imposter syndrome. When I was writing up my PhD, a colleague recommended me for a postdoctoral position. When I say 'writing up my PhD', I mean I had to work through the grief of a miscarriage first by painting the entire inside of our house, cleaning the house and purchasing a new desk chair before I could even get started. I think five months was quite speedy given the extent of my procrastination. Although it was my CV and credentials, and I was the one who showed up for the interview, it felt like the only reason I got the position was because of my contact, rather than my expertise or skills. It left me desperately needing to prove myself and seek reassurance to the unvoiced thought, 'Please tell me you made the right choice.'

Even when I did feel competent in an area, there was always a part of my role where I felt like I didn't know enough. It was particularly difficult at the start because I was making the transition from my comfort zone of organometallic chemistry to carbohydrate chemistry. While they sound similar, the similarities end with the nomenclature. I devoured books and papers every waking moment, not because of a compelling interest in the subject, but just to find solid ground, because at any second I was going to be found out. Have you ever experienced the first layer of imposter syndrome, that feeling you are going to get found out, whether in the past or right now?

The second layer of imposter syndrome is over-crediting others. If someone tries to give us even the tiniest hint of praise, we can't take it. Instead, we treat it like the Oscars and say, 'I couldn't have done it without this person, and this person, and this person.' We need to give recognition where it is rightly due, as well as being explicit in claiming our part. We shine a light on others, and train people to look away from us. Over time, we start to feel resentful, isolated, or in extreme cases, worthless. Think of an example when you over-credited others. How did this impact you in both the short and long term?

The third layer of imposter syndrome is using minimising language. I was often heard saying to my friends 'literally anyone can do a PhD' even though, according to the Education at a Glance 2021 report by the Organisation for Economic Co-operation and Development, on average only 1% of those aged twenty-five to sixty-four hold one.[11] We say 'it was no big thing', 'it was good', but not 'it was novel', 'it was great' or 'groundbreaking'. When we listen to our own internal rhetoric, and tune into that radio station over days, weeks, months or even years, we start to believe it as the one and only truth. Reflect for yourself, is your self-talk more positive or negative?

Now when I give my own bestselling imposter syndrome workshop, The Psychology of Selves: Beyond imposter syndrome, I find that the overwhelming majority of participants already know the term. It has become part of our lexicon. In Michelle Obama's number one international bestselling book *Becoming*, she writes about putting her head down and letting her work speak for itself; about feeling like she had something to prove because of the colour of her skin and the shape of her body.[12]

When I'm invited as a keynote speaker at conferences, senior leaders love to regale the audience with their stories of imposter syndrome in an attempt to make us all feel less alone in our struggles. On one hand, these stories are inspiring and there is solace in knowing you are not alone. On the other hand, you are witnessing just how competent they are, how they overcame imposter syndrome and therefore they are not like you, the *real* imposter.

I've sat in those conferences thinking to myself, 'You weren't paralysed by fear and avoiding public speaking at all costs for a decade, negatively shaping your whole career. Your imposter syndrome must have been different from mine because you just don't seem to get what it's like.' That's because the real problem isn't imposter syndrome. The real problem lies beneath.

What lies beneath

Imposter syndrome is used as a blanket term to cover a multitude of symptoms and behaviours. It's like looking at the tip of an iceberg and saying 'that's a big iceberg' when the largest part of the iceberg is underneath the water's surface. If a client is struggling with saying no, or setting and maintaining boundaries with their manager, I will resource them with nonconfrontational conversation templates to support achieving a different outcome.

Even more frustrating is finding the courage to speak up and advocate for oneself, but without the conviction, we are often not heard or respected. Without getting to the root of the issue, it doesn't matter how many nonconfrontational conversations you have, those situations will keep presenting themselves and replaying again and again. That's why getting to the core of what's going on is my key focus. We need to work out why those situations occur in the first place, so that the presenting problem disappears faster than you can say 'liquid nitrogen at room temperature'. (Liquid nitrogen boils into nitrogen vapour at room temperature and pressure. It has many uses beyond keeping things cool from instant ice cream to levitation.)

I've seen imposter syndrome originating from three different places. Number one is family and behavioural patterns developed in early childhood. If as a child you experience trauma, without the right support it can have devastating long-term physical, behavioural or psychological consequences. Some effects include: physical health problems, chronic illnesses, mental health issues, difficulties maintaining friendships and relationships, unhealthy coping strategies, and challenges coping with work pressures. Even the most positive of parenting situations can produce little imposters. When children are praised for sporting, academic or musical achievements, they feel loved. To feel more loved, they must achieve more, and that's the route to creating overachievers. (By definition, if you have a PhD, you are already an overachiever.)

The second origin source comes from specific incidents that trigger limiting beliefs or emotions. When I was in the third year of my master's in chemistry, we had to complete a lab-based project. The final oral presentation of the research accounted for 10% of the overall mark. As I walked into the room, two eminent professors sat together laughing and joking. I set up my slides and had my notecards. I was ready, but it felt like they didn't even know I was there. When they finally did acknowledge my presence they said, 'Put all your notes down and talk to us about what you did.' I was completely thrown. The adrenaline pumped through my veins, my heart was pounding and I had no executive brain function, just legs that wanted to run away but remained rooted to the spot. This was an immediate, overwhelming emotional response, which was disproportionate to the situation because my brain had interpreted the trigger as a significant threat. My body was behaving like my life was in danger when it was not, and all I could manage was one-word answers so I could get out of there as fast as possible and get my brain and body back under control.

That experience led me to believe I was no good at public speaking of any kind. There was probably something wrong with me. In fact, it was better if I didn't speak up at all. It negatively shaped the next decade of my career, as I would do anything to avoid the spotlight.

The third reason is often harder to identify because it is the soup we are swimming in. This could be environmental, cultural, institutional or privilege-based discrimination. For example, when I was facilitating a workshop in a London-based corporate, a Taiwanese member of staff told me that when they went for their interview the whole panel of five were white. She believed they only hired her to tick the DEI box because of her ethnicity. When they actively listen to her in meetings, she believes it's because, 'I'm the only brown face in the room and they are being polite, but don't really think I have anything of value to say.'

Take a moment to reflect. What layers of imposter syndrome have you experienced, right now or in the past? Can you pinpoint any of the origin sources of your imposter syndrome? This information will be a helpful data set when we start to decode these imposter syndrome behaviours using my VOICE methodology.

Flavours of fear – one scoop or two?

At the core of all the reasons why we might feel imposter syndrome, and therefore many of the challenges we face in life and our careers, is fear. Think of fear as the different flavours of ice cream. Fear of feeling fear itself, fear of being unloved, fear of failure, fear of not being good enough, fear of being alone, fear of something being wrong or even of feeling you are wrong in some way. One scoop or two for you? It's time to change our relationship with fear.

The parable of the arrow is a well-known Buddhist story from the Sallatha Sutta.[13] If a person is struck by an arrow, that must be painful. The second arrow is when the person wishes not to have been struck in the first place. They berate themselves for being in the wrong place at the wrong time, get angry with the person who shot them, or feel sorry for themself. We can't always control the first arrow. Loved ones unfortunately die, miscarriages do happen, people are discriminated against, bullied and made redundant. But the second arrow is our reaction to the first. The second arrow is optional, and the worst part is, it's self-inflicted.

Learning how to accept our external challenges and inner emotional landscape just as they are stops us from suffering over what is. Surely some situations and emotions are painful enough, without adding the second arrow of suffering on top?[14] Notice how this relates to your current challenges in life.

Newton's third law of motion proposes whenever two objects interact, they exert equal and opposite forces on each other.[15] If you are not in acceptance of your fears, then you are resisting the thing that is going to set you free. When you can accept your feelings without trying to get away from them, you can move through those feelings, and they can be released more easily, or you can take action to change something – the equivalent of being able to expose the iceberg as a whole and marvel at its exquisite crystalline beauty.

There is lightness in our shadows. There are gifts to be uncovered. Start right now by pinpointing emotions you hate to feel; the emotions you put up walls against, avoid, numb, swallow or put on a shelf so you can disconnect from them, so you don't have to feel them fully. Your emotional allergies.

The issue is, you can't selectively numb emotions.[16] Think of emotions like a trapdoor. If you stuff shame, hurt, sadness, anger, grief or fear under the trapdoor, you can numb them a little, but they are always there, seeping, oozing or even exploding out of the cracks in the woodwork. If you put the lid on those feelings you hate to feel, you are also trapping in other emotions like joy, happiness, love, excitement, peace and fulfilment. You feel neither so bad you can't get out of bed nor the high of the emotional roller coaster. It's like a heart monitor no longer signalling, emotions flatlining.

Just be your selves

Dr Hal Stone and Dr Sidra Stone are exceptional psychologists; sadly Hal passed away in 2020. They were the originators of the Voice Dialogue methodology and the Psychology of Selves.[17] I was lucky enough to train under the instruction of Annie Stoker in 2021/2022, who worked with them along with Michael Rowland for ten years. I want to be clear that Voice Dialogue is not the only access point to understanding selves, there are other modalities too, such as Shirzad Chamine's Positive Intelligence,[18] Gabor Maté's Compassionate Inquiry methodology,[19] and Richard Schwartz's Internal Family Systems.[20] Eckhart Tolle himself,[21] plus many others, speak of these discrete 'selves' within us. It is my deepest wish that you, too, find an access point as resonant as I did.

Essentially, most people hear different voices or 'selves' in their heads. This is perfectly normal. We move seamlessly between these modes every day, and we use this terminology in everyday life. One self says, 'Go for a walk at lunchtime,' and another self says, 'You must sit at your desk with lunch and go through your email inbox before it gets completely out of control. People are waiting for you to respond.' Which voice is strongest determines which action you will take. Do you notice these different and sometimes seemingly conflicting voices?

As a child, you experiment with many selves depending on a number of different factors: the stability and safety within the family situation, the familial, cultural or implicit expectations, the native culture, the number of children and the personalities of those children in the family, as well as any other influencing criteria. What is safest for survival determines which handful of selves become the strongest selves and the primary self-system, the ones which will be used most frequently. The following selves tipped into the unhelpful range of characteristics are the ones I see time and again in clients who are experiencing eroded confidence or lacking in self-esteem.

The Pusher

Are you always busy, busy, busy, with a long list of things to do? Always thinking about what you should do, must do or need to do? Working longer and harder than everyone else to succeed, with the added benefit of being so busy that you don't have any time to really feel how you are feeling? Emotions are squished ('There's no time for emotions right now,' says the Pusher, 'there are things that need doing'), boundaries get blurred, exhaustion is masked, resentment is rife and feels like a bitter pill you have swallowed. Slowing down, resting or being a failure breaks the rules of the Pusher. Do you have a first-class Pusher in you?

The Perfectionist

The Perfectionist is the self that is setting the standards. Do you like things to be perfect? To be strictly on time because otherwise you feel nervous? The Perfectionist is the part that likes the house spotless, and dislikes doing things unless you can do them perfectly. The Perfectionist hates mess, chaos, spontaneity or being caught at home with dishes in the sink. In the work context, the Perfectionist can team up with the Pusher to have you working extra hard to make sure the work is of the 'right' standard. There's only you that can do it properly, right? The Perfectionist seeks to meticulously and exaggeratedly overprepare beyond what's healthy, desperately trying to find solid ground to rule out that possibility of not being good enough or not doing something well enough, or even of being wrong. Conversely, your Perfectionist may team up with the Protector Controller and slip you into procrastination, or avoidance techniques. If you don't get started on something (like tackling an email which you know contains lots of feedback), then you get to avoid those uncomfortable feelings for a little longer. Feeling substandard breaks the rules of the Perfectionist.

The Pleaser

This is the self that wants to please people and places a lot of weight on what people are thinking and saying about you. The Pleaser wants everyone to be happy and for people to think you are nice. Do you say yes automatically when someone asks you to do something, even if you don't want to? Do you dislike saying no, conflicts or arguments, or people being angry with you? To really discover your Pleaser at work, ask yourself, 'What am I doing, that I don't want to be doing?' and 'What am I not doing, that I want to do?' If you can answer these questions, the Pleaser is currently running your life. Displeasing someone breaks the rules of the Pleaser. Can all the Pleasers reading this please raise your hand.

The Protector Controller

Do you like to feel safe and comfortable no matter what? To be in control and certain of the outcomes? Do you dislike new situations, threats or discomfort of any sort? As Dr Shefali writes in *A Radical Awakening*, 'Pleasers want to show the world how good they are, whereas controllers want to show the world just how competent they are. Both are ruled by a morbid unconscious desire to answer the burning internal question, 'Am I good enough?' They quench their anxiety that they aren't good enough by channelling this frenetic energy into controlling everything in their sight.'[22] Feeling vulnerable, hurt or scared breaks the rules of the Protector Controller.

The Rule-maker

Do you like everything to be done a certain way, for everyone to behave according to the 'rules', even if you don't follow them? This is the self that worries about all the possible consequences of your actions and talks in terms of 'shoulds', 'musts' and 'have tos'. Strong Rule-makers cause all-or-nothing thinking, intolerance, judgement and rigidity. They feel somewhat superior to and better than others.

The Inner Critic

We've touched on this before, but it's the self that tells you off, feels like you are never doing well enough, and focuses on your faults and weaknesses. It compares you unfavourably to other people and has you feeling less than others. The Inner Critic's sole purpose is to criticise you into being perfect, and it goes about things in a self-destructive way, often using words and phrases from your boss, partner, mum, dad, siblings, friends or colleagues that feel hurtful. In extreme cases, if the voice gets too strong and out of control, it can become a Killer Critic and even result in suicide. Even at a minor level the Inner Critic is debilitating. This self has a special relationship with all of the other selves. It serves as a police officer, checking to see if you are abiding by the selves' rules. If you break a rule, the Inner Critic will step in to castigate you, beating you up with your own thoughts. It is terrified of being shamed by others and so monitors all your behaviour to avoid this. The Rule-maker supports the notion that you are 'better than' others, whereas the Inner Critic has you firmly set in the belief you are 'less than'. It is possible to have both the Inner Critic and the Rule-maker in the unhelpful range at the same time.

The tip of the iceberg

Each of the different selves masks an emotion, a feeling you are trying hard to avoid (an emotional allergy). The way in which a self does this is by building a tower of behaviours over the top of the emotion in an attempt to minimise the intensity of the feeling. It's these towers that are the surface part of that imposter syndrome iceberg, the armour we present to the world that prevents us from being our true and authentic selves and robs us of the ability to fully express who we are.

CLIENT STORY
Dr Verena Wolfram – building towers of behaviours

Verena was frustrated with her level of achievement at work, failing to progress through internal promotions. She regularly checked on LinkedIn what others in her graduation year were doing and compared herself unfavourably. She felt like she was massively falling short of her true potential. English wasn't her primary language, and she would berate her language skills for being the reason why she was passed over at interview stage. It was severely affecting her sense of self and her confidence levels.

Having attended one of the Oxbridge colleges, Verena excelled academically. When she started her PhD, she believed she would go all the way to becoming a professor and win a Nobel prize. She certainly had the potential, but she didn't yield enough papers in her first postdoc. Her second postdoc coincided with making choices about starting a family, and she sacrificed her own academic career to support her partner's progression.

When I started working with Verena, she was an assessment analyst at the National Institute for Health and Care Excellence (NICE), and she had a persistent belief she must get to the top as quickly as possible: the corporate equivalent of becoming a professor and winning a Nobel prize. Just like in academia, she had reached the point of feeling like a failure for being in the same role for three years. It was a feeling she was uncomfortable with.

Her emotional allergy was the fear of failure, and to protect herself from that feeling she had built different towers of behaviours on top of the fear to squash it deep down inside. Avoidance of feelings through productivity and overworking: the Pusher. Over-giving to keep everyone happy, receive praise and avoid conflict: the Pleaser. Operating with high standards, and judging others for not having those standards: the Perfectionist, with a side helping of the Rule-maker. Avoiding activities that could result in failure or feeling inadequate: the Protector Controller.

Through our work together, Verena learned how to separate from the agendas of these discrete parts of herself, and how to manage her internal vulnerability and increase her levels of tolerance to the fear of failure. This resulted in gaining access to more of what she was looking for: strong work–life boundaries, feeling confident and capable, and not worrying about what other people think.

Fear-based armour versus authentic inner confidence

Instead of striving to climb the career ladder to reach the top, she uncovered what would make her truly happy. Verena was successful in a twelve-month internal secondment as a technical advisor in the Office for Digital Health at NICE, which was more aligned with her natural talents and happened to also be a more senior position with a pay rise. At the end of her sabbatical, she successfully pivoted to senior medical affairs manager of scientific engagement at Pfizer, whose mission would make her feel more fulfilled. This time, she wasn't hampered by worrying if she was sounding eloquent in her use of the English language. Instead, as her true and authentic self, she was the first choice.

 Listen to Verena's full podcast episode at **https:// hannahnikeroberts.com/inspiring-stories-021- verena-wolfram.**

It's important to remember that these selves are not negative, they all have strengths and weaknesses. For example, without the Pleaser, you would struggle to have any functional relationships. Problems arise when they are too prominent, too strong. Like a dial set too high, that's when the selves' behaviours tip into the unhelpful range. The Inner Critic, in and of itself, is not a problem. It's there to keep you on your toes and to help you reach your full potential. It only becomes a problem in the unhelpful range, where its toxic language can berate you until you feel utterly miserable.

Reflect on which of these different selves you recognise in yourself as being strong. I call these your stress tag team.

CLIENT STORY
Dr Jane Doherty – attachment versus authenticity

A client of mine, Dr Jane Doherty, was born into challenging family dynamics. Her elder sister was more of a natural rebel. Jane witnessed her sister's rebellious behaviour coming under fire from her parents, so she conformed to their expectations. She became the 'good girl', which meant love was given with conditions.

Attachment means attaching to a parent or caregiver because without them you would not get food or shelter and would not survive. Authenticity is being in touch with gut feelings, being able to listen to the gut response which alerts you to danger. If the gut response is that the parent or caregiver is scary in some way, the child will want to run away. A small child can't survive alone, and therefore the need to attach trumps authenticity. To maintain survival through attachment with her parents, Jane had to concede her authenticity. Please note that 'scary' means different things to an individual's nervous system. Scary might be aggressive, violent or abusive behaviour, but to a highly sensitive person, scary could mean being told off, looked at disapprovingly or sensing unease in silence – all of which can be internalised similarly.[23]

Jane let go of her preferences and desires, which manifested as a lack of ability to fully express herself, grab life with both hands, do the things she wanted to do, say the things she wanted to say. When not conforming to those original expectations, Jane would feel the uncomfortable feelings of shame and guilt.

Paradoxically, she also felt these for not being authentic to herself. Over time, she learned how to squash her feelings deep inside and disconnect from them. We can't selectively numb emotions, so Jane became detached from her full range of emotional dexterity, including feelings of fulfilment and happiness.

As Jane's career progressed, it became her parents' expectation that she should stay on the academic path. The unwritten rule was that she must not perform lower than her uncle. There was a perceived favouritism for Jane's uncle in the wider family and Jane was often compared unfavourably to him, as he had to be seen as the most successful person on a scientific path in the family. Her parents' way of responding was to retaliate and play into this instead of protecting her, making Jane a pawn in a family game of chess.

For Jane, this resulted in a strong Inner Critic voice as well as towers of Pleaser, Pusher and Perfectionist behaviours, built to suppress the icky emotions of shame and guilt. There was a real fear of parental rejection if she gave up working in an academic setting. It was a huge win when she forged her own pathway beyond academic research. More importantly, she began learning how to reconnect her brain, body and emotions. When strong selves are running the show, it often feels like there is no choice, we are powerless. Once Jane's more vulnerable selves knew she could handle her emotions, they could relax and give her more space and, ultimately, the freedom of choice.

As my mentor Annie Stoker likes to say, when you are avoiding emotional allergies by building towers of selves, it's like playing 'Chopsticks' on the piano – banging away with the same four keys, hoping a different tune will emerge. When you learn to identify your different selves and separate from their agendas, you can regain choice in your behaviours and actions. Imagine becoming the CEO of your own boardroom of selves; being able to listen to an opinion without believing it is the one and only truth; having the awareness to choose a new perspective or how you would like to respond. Imagine that. It's like regaining all eighty-eight keys on the piano. Finally, chopsticks can become Chopin.

IMPLEMENT THIS

Journal on the following questions:

- What layers of imposter syndrome have you experienced?
- Can you pinpoint any of the origin sources of your imposter syndrome?
- Reflect on the different selves. Which of the stress tag team do you recognise in yourself as being strong: the Pusher, Pleaser, Perfectionist, Protector Controller, Rule-maker or Inner Critic?

5
Rebalancing To Wholeness Using The VOICE Framework

If you have selves that are in the unhelpful range, they have become overactive for a reason. Towers of selves find both primitive and creatively elaborate ways to cover up the feelings you are fighting so hard not to feel, the vulnerability inside. When this occurs, you are not living a life, you are living a pattern. I have experienced for myself and seen in my clients that everything we are looking for is on the other side of meeting and partnering with our vulnerability. This means not labelling yourself as 'bad' and 'wrong' for being the way you are, but accepting who you *really* are and remaining open when all you want to do is close down and get into defence mode.

You can continue to avoid vulnerability by enlisting your Rule-maker to make everything black and white, good or bad, the uncertain, certain, but this will constrain and restrict your potential. Let that approach go, and discover that fully embracing vulnerability is the key to unlocking your trapdoor of emotional allergies – the place joy, intimacy, love and fulfilment have also been hiding.

Brené Brown put vulnerability on the map in her 2010 TED Talk, 'The Power of Vulnerability'.[1] In her recent book, *Atlas of the Heart*, she describes vulnerability as the emotion we experience during times of uncertainty, risk and emotional exposure.[2] Vulnerability is not weakness. It requires even more strength to hold a mirror to yourself than it does to cover up with masks, armour and towers of behaviours. Being your true and authentic self is not an easy, comfortable path. If it was, everyone would be doing it. The fact that you are here and reading this book indicates that you want things to be different. I'm not asking you to do this alone, but to lean in to being supported. The question is, will you face your vulnerability? Are you all in?

Being all in means building awareness of the selves that are currently running the show. Once you uncover and manage the underlying vulnerability and root cause of your emotions and behaviours, you gain separation from these selves and move them back into a helpful range. In the process, you gain access to more of what you are looking for: perhaps to 'be a human being, not a human doing' as the Dalai Lama says,[3] or to be confident, to shine when speaking, to feel welcome and wanted in a group, or even to enjoy and be fully present in new situations without needing to control them. Whatever you would like a little more of, welcome it into the world of new possibilities.

If you continue to squash those feelings down and develop more extreme behaviours to keep the trapdoor on those emotions shut, without support, eventually the trapdoor will not be able to hold the pressure. Rather than reaching full-blown burnout, anxiety that morphs into panic attacks, or depression, make the changes that need to happen now. As a coach, it is my job to help clients unlock their latent potential. I want to share with you the VOICE methodology I use to help my clients restore eroded confidence and move towards authentic wholeness.

V: Verifying triggers

Put in its simplest terms, a trigger is something that causes an intense, and usually uncomfortable and unwanted, emotional reaction. Can you think of three people, organisations, animals or films you disapprove of, can't stand or just plain hate? Ask yourself, 'What is the quality they have that I dislike?' 'How do I like to be instead?' For example, I hate spiders because they are unpredictable. You never know if a daddy-long-legs is going to fly at you, go up the wall or under the bed, or do something bizarre. I like things to be predictable. In this example, we could hazard a guess that I have a strong Rule-maker, because when we live by a set of rules, things become ordered and predictable. While we can rationalise that this is a good thing, if my Rule-maker was in the unhelpful range, the need to be ordered and for things to be predictable could squash spontaneity and creativity, and result in rigid all-or-nothing thinking.

The second type of trigger is limiting beliefs, thoughts we hold to be true that limit our experience of life. Some classic examples of belief systems from my clients include: 'I'm not good enough', 'I don't know enough', 'I'm not capable enough', 'I'm not worthy', 'people are dangerous' and 'people are disappointing'. In the expression 'I would like to X, but . . .', the thing that comes after the 'but' is a limiting belief. Even 'I've not got enough time' can be a limiting belief. I used to say this to myself a lot, then I realised everyone in the world has twenty-four hours in a day. When I say I haven't got enough time, what I'm really saying is that this thing is currently not a priority for me.

Limiting beliefs become problematic because they stop you from acting and have you stuck in procrastination. They have you taking actions that go against your values and your authenticity, and they cause untold unhappiness.

The third type of triggers are sisterhood and cultural wounds. They have us feeling alone in a room full of people, that we don't fit in or belong, that we are different from everyone else or may have even been othered. Think about your answers to the following questions:

1. What triggers you in a group situation?

2. What triggers you about your mum/sister?

3. What triggers you about groups of women?

Explore each trigger with compassion for yourself, like a ball of wool that you are gently untangling. If at any time the process becomes too much, take a break, return to it later or reach out for further support.

The fourth type of trigger occurs when we let go of our basic needs, such as food, water, sleep, movement, connection and alone time. I once received a work phone call when I was on a day off with my young son. I said yes to everything requested of me, but as soon as I put the phone down, I cried. It wasn't about the request; I was more than capable of achieving the outcomes. I was exhausted due to lack of sleep, and had therefore slipped into an under-resourced state. The request simply tipped me over the edge. Are there any basic needs that you know you are consistently not meeting, which could be contributing to your triggers? What actions can you take to improve how you respond to these needs?

O: Opportunities to release limitations

To release limiting beliefs or emotions, we first have to identify them. One of the problems my clients often report is feeling triggered and destabilised by certain people. Usually, these people will be strong characters – confrontational, or even aggressive in their approach – or the person will be in a position hierarchically above them.

Destabilisation takes the form of pre-empting the situation, running through all of the what-ifs, such as

'What if this happens; then what?', until the worst-case scenario becomes a perceived inevitability. Sometimes the worry unfolds during a situation; for example, worrying so much about what to say in a meeting it takes away from being fully present, which makes responding in the moment more challenging. My personal nemesis is rumination: going over and over a situation in your mind after it has occurred, being preoccupied with interpreting what happened, often to the point of catastrophe. The problem with all of this is the inordinate amount of time and energy it takes, alongside being consumed by the thoughts and therefore not fully present in life.

It can often feel like the destabilising person has negative intentions towards you. What if our default was to assume people have inherently good intentions towards us? That they are doing the best they can, with the resources available to them at that time? Believing this doesn't mean people will behave differently, but their behaviour is easier to handle when we know they are doing their best with the life experiences they have had and their current level of awareness and personal development.

Most likely though, the destabilisation does not originate in the form of power plays from other people; it is an internal conflict within us.

It was 2017, and I was enjoying being on holiday with a group of friends when I overheard snippets of conversations along the lines of, 'Wouldn't it be great to all go on holiday again next year?' I saw my friend shushing the speaker. In that moment, I believed it was because they all wanted to go on holiday without me. Why else would you shush someone? I felt rejected and upset. I ruminated on that moment, not intensely, but it was on my mind on and off for a couple of weeks. With all the personal development work I have done, I could see what I was doing to myself.

In *Man's Search for Meaning*, Victor Frankl states: 'Between stimulus and response, there is a space. In that space is our power to choose our response. In our response lies our growth and freedom.'[4] In my choice of response I was making up my own elaborate story, and the only truth within it all was that I was on holiday with my friends. Everything else was a story attached to that one truth. Rather than feeling hurt and rejected, and pulling away from the friendship, I decided to speak to my friend about what I had seen and heard. Addressing concerns head on can transform the integrity of relationships. Yes, everyone loved the holiday as much as me and wanted to repeat it. They would never go on a friends' holiday without inviting me, and as for the shush? Who knows? Perhaps it was the movement of arms batting away a flying insect. It could have been anything, but certainly wasn't my version of reality. That conversation brought us even closer together, and made me realise the importance of seeing thoughts as neutral events, of choosing which thoughts to follow, and when we do happen to follow a thought that triggers a cascade of unhelpful story creation, of being able to see it for what it is and challenge that story with objective reality: the truth.

We are always in a moment of interpretation, so most of our thoughts aren't the truth. A moment occurs and we make meaning out of that moment based on several different inputs. Next time you are triggered, take some time to work through each of the following input criteria in turn, and see if this creates a new-found awareness of being able to actively choose your response.

Body

Have you met your basic need for sleep, water, food, exercise, alone time and connection time? I know after a lack of sleep I will have a much more negative outlook than when I've had eight hours of sleep and am feeling epic.

The central message in Gina Rippon's book *The Gendered Brain: The new neuroscience that shatters the myth of the female brain* is that a gendered world will produce a gendered brain.[5] Her book stands with Angela Saini's *Inferior* and Cordelia Fine's *Delusions of Gender* in rooting out the neurosexism that has pervaded attempts to understand difference at the brain level.[6] This is the practice of claiming there are fixed differences between female and male brains that explain certain gendered characteristics. Not wanting to deliberately reinforce harmful gender stereotypes, with caution, I add Dr Louann Brizendine's hypothesis. In her book *The Female Brain,* she reports that when faced with the same situation at different phases of our menstrual cycle we will interpret them differently.[7] If you are naturally cycling, the most important time to consider is around a week before menstruation. Progesterone and oestrogen plummet, testosterone falls rapidly slightly later, and the net result is a feeling of being on edge, and needing everything to be decided, cleared and sorted. This is different to our ovulation phase when oestrogen and testosterone peak, progesterone is climbing, and all is well with the world. Cycles are individual and subjective, so do take the time to tune into your body and notice your rhythm and any differences in your thinking and outlook during different phases. You might be surprised at what you discover.

Our emotional allergies have a huge impact on how our body and mind will interpret situations, and therefore the selves which show up to manage them.

Mind

If the moment in question causes a conflict with our values, then we will naturally create a negative story association. I have a strong value for integrity, and if someone asks me to do something that lacks integrity, I can't do it. I start to feel paralysed and worry about all of the what-ifs.

One of the biggest inputs in the mind is the limiting beliefs we hold about ourselves. In fact, specific selves can be the torch bearers of these limiting beliefs. If your limiting beliefs are exposed, your mind will find evidence to back them up, attaching emotional allergies and sending you down the road of suffering.

Connection

A strong religious or spiritual connection can cause conflicts between the situation and the belief system, or have us interpret the world through a certain lens.

We quickly attach an emotion to the meaning we create, and then take action based on how we think and feel about ourselves. The cycle is continuous, which is why just one moment can result in negativity escalating over several hours or days, and could manifest as a perceived character trait and a habit of a lifetime. Take yourself back to the last time you were overthinking. How long did you spend in thought before you were able to come back to the present moment?

I: Integrating new approaches

Every thought is a decision point. It is a choice. The choice to continue down the path of pre-empting, worrying or ruminating, or the choice to challenge that thought with the truth. The truth is literal and always short: I'm responding to my email, I'm going to dance class for the first time in twenty years, I'm in a meeting, or in my case, sitting around the swimming pool on holiday. Everything else is the story attached to this truth. Try challenging the story yourself, and if you can't separate out the truth, find someone else to help you do that. It might be helpful to ask yourself the four questions that can genuinely change your life devised by Byron Katie:[8]

1. Is it true?

2. Can you absolutely know it is true? (Usually, the word 'absolutely' will stop the story in its tracks.)

3. How do you react and what happens when you believe that thought?

4. Who would you be without the thought?

You might be pleasantly surprised with the results. Once the thought is challenged, you can have a great day ahead, rather than be pulled into the spiral of negativity.

It's not enough to just think our way out of the cycle, we must feel our way out too. In the book *Burnout* by sisters Emily and Amelia Nagoski, the authors talk about the need to complete the emotional stress cycle.[9] If you were chased by an escaped tiger from a zoo, for example, it would trigger one of the following stress responses: fight, flight, freeze, fawn or flop. If the zookeeper caught the tiger and removed the threat, would that mean that the adrenaline and cortisol coursing through your body suddenly disappeared? Of course not. We have to actively do something to release emotions and get back to homeostasis.

If a fox chases a rabbit, and the rabbit is lucky enough to escape, you will notice that the rabbit shakes to release the adrenaline, and then returns to eating grass as if the last few minutes never happened. We can achieve the same return to equilibrium if we are experiencing fear, anxiety or panic by literally shaking it out. Take each part of your body in turn and shake it. (For best effect try doing this to some African drumming music.)

If the emotion to be released is anger, jealousy or envy, try rolling up a clean towel, putting it between your teeth and screaming. You will feel your stomach contracting and a sensation of getting the anger out of your body. Punching a pillow works well too. One of my clients, Dr Natasha Rhys, even bought a baseball bat for hitting her mattress and sofa cushions. Much healthier than keeping her emotions bottled up inside and damaging her internal system, or punching someone in the face.

 You can listen to Natasha's full story at **https:// hannahnikeroberts.com/inspiring-stories-025- dr-natasha-rhys.**

Studies published in *Frontiers in Psychology* have identified anger as being a secondary emotion that masks the primary emotion.[10] Often, underneath all of the anger, is a lot of hurt and upset. Do be prepared for that. Crying is your body's natural way of releasing, so give yourself permission to do so when you are experiencing sadness, upset, hurt or grief. If you are struggling to connect with the emotion, music can be a powerful access point, and I've always found watching the film *Little Women* will crack you wide open.

Any change of state will help. Go from inside to outside, from being static to moving. Do not stay stuck in the tunnel of unprocessed emotions. You must come out of the other end and complete the stress cycle. What's the alternative here? Do you really want to hold onto the emotion for years, even decades?

If you are thinking, 'This is just how I am, I'm an anxious person so this will not work for me,' or 'I've done work on this in the past, and how I am is the best I can hope for,' it's time to rethink that assumption. Ask yourself, when did you decide you were an anxious person? Was there ever a time that wasn't the truth? Challenge yourself. Were you anxious even as a baby? What is the consequence of you believing this is a character trait rather than a behaviour which can be changed? If you believed wholeheartedly that you were safe, worthy and enough, what would happen in those moments instead?

Pre-empting, worrying and ruminating are symptoms of overthinking, which can become a habitual way of being if not challenged. I know this first-hand, and when I started using the technique of challenging my stories with the absolute truth, I needed to use it a lot. More recently, I can only think of two situations that I had to challenge using this technique, which shows how, over time, the process becomes unconscious.

Your thoughts shape your reality and how you feel about yourself. To change those self-sabotaging stories, you need to start with awareness; no behavioural change can proceed without it. Begin by being aware of the problem itself. Then you will be able to catch yourself in the act of a numbing, defensive or self-sabotaging behaviour. Finally, you can decode the triggers to the origin point and be so self-aware you have a choice in, or preceding, the moment itself to choose your response and experience a spiral of growth: awareness-release-growth. Then you are stood in a completely new place able to uncover your next level awareness.

C: Challenging conversations

Did you go to the lesson at school which taught you how to ask for what you need, say no gracefully, delegate effectively, and set and maintain your boundaries? I thought not. Why are we not teaching these important skills alongside academic subjects?

CLIENT STORY
Dr Joanne Taylor – Boundary Lines

When I first started working with Joanne, she was consistently clocking a sixty-plus-hour week, and feeling stressed and underappreciated for all that hard work. One of her main intentions was to change her working habits to have more time and energy for life and her relationship. In one session, I asked Joanne to draw a circle and write the names of all the people she was willing to go into energy deficit for, if they asked for her help. In another circle I asked her to write the names of all the people she cared about but was not willing to self-sacrifice for if she didn't have enough time or energy to give.

This exercise highlighted over 100 people she was consistently self-sacrificing for, including her colleagues and line manager; for example, by not finishing lunch, not taking a break, and staying late to help others with their priorities. It took its toll, as you can't give, give and give some more without consequences. She was like a phone battery in the red with no energy socket to recharge.

Based on this realisation, Joanne made a list of all the people she was consciously willing to go into energy deficit for. There were five people in that circle. She drew the boundary line, metaphorically moved all the other people across the line, and learned how to reclaim her space and say no. The boundary was set between what was OK and what was not OK, for her.

Things changed rapidly after that session. Joanne implemented a new calendar system which restricted when people could book time with her. She left the building to take breaks and got home by 5.30pm to ensure quality time with her partner, and time to exercise was reinstated. Not only that, the process had a profound impact on her career. You would think working less would mean saying goodbye to her chances of promotion, right? Wrong. Within six months of implementing these changes, Joanne was promoted and upgraded in salary.

What have you discovered for yourself about where your time and energy are going? How will you start to protect your energy and get the right people in the right circles, so you consciously know and defend your boundary lines?

E: Expressing authenticity

For me, being in a position of integrity with yourself is when what you think, say, do and feel are in sync. It is a process of peeling back the layers of what's not serving you and opening yourself up to more. What else can you uncover about yourself and your talents when you're no longer hiding and numbing yourself with Netflix? Once you have verified your triggers, found opportunities to release your personal limitations, and integrated new approaches, you are already beginning to express your true and authentic self.

Now, answer the following two questions:

1. If you weren't paralysed by the fear of messing it up, being disappointed, of making the wrong decision, what would you go for?

2. If the quality of your life while you were going for it mattered the most, how would you go for it? It's not just *what* we do, it's *who* we are while we do it that matters.

In 2017, Alex Honnold did what even the world's best rock climbers thought was impossible. He climbed to the top of El Capitan, a granite rock mountain more than 3,000 feet high, without a rope, harness or net.[11] His feat was showcased in the Oscar-winning documentary *Free Solo*.[12] Neuroscientists were so fascinated by Alex's ability to handle fear, they convinced him to let them conduct some tests on his brain.

They scanned Alex using functional magnetic resonance imaging while flashing a series of images at him. Usually, fear-based images would activate the amygdala, the brain's processing centre for rewarding and painful events,[13] but in Alex's case this didn't happen. Alex believes he has trained his brain to detect real threats more acutely. He says in a podcast recording, 'It seemed perfectly natural that my amygdala wouldn't trigger while looking at pictures lying in a metal tube, because I'm totally safe.'[14]

It gets more thought-provoking. The media became interested in Alex's success, which thrust him into public speaking, including the opportunity to give a TED Talk.[15] You might hypothesise he would have no problem delivering the talk because it's not life or death, but the opposite was true. He described shaking behind the stage in anticipation of what was going to happen next, validating the statistic from the National Institute of Mental Health that 75% of people are more afraid of public speaking than death.[16] Jerry Seinfeld retorts, 'This means to the average person, if you go to a funeral, you're better off in the casket than doing the eulogy.'[17]

There is a case for starting small and building on your successes. Alex may have benefitted from speaking on some smaller stages first – the equivalent of a Perfectionist being OK with leaving a towel on the floor for a couple of hours. In fact, he went on tour after the TED Talk, and had to speak so much he successfully desensitised himself to his fear of public speaking.

I thought Alex's experience was interesting, because everyone has their own arch nemesis when it comes to the flavour of emotions they hate to feel. I want you to think about when you feel most vulnerable. What is one tiny step you can take to get more comfortable with the uncomfortable? Over time, stretch the boundaries of this comfort zone until you can be present and OK with expressing what you built all of those towers of behaviours on top of, the emotion you were keeping under wraps in the first place. Once you can do this, you are moving towards wholeness and your true authenticity. These are the steps you need to take to unlock a well of potential inside you that you didn't know existed, and the ability to design a career for fulfilment rather than a career to avoid failure.

IMPLEMENT THIS

Rebalance to wholeness using the VOICE framework:

- Identify and verify your triggers, whether they take the form of your different selves, limiting beliefs, sisterhood or cultural wounds, or not meeting your basic needs.

- Look for opportunities to release limitations and build awareness.

- Integrate new approaches by separating the truth from the story and releasing emotions.

- Have the conversations you find challenging, and aim to understand and protect your boundaries.

- Express your authenticity, pinpoint your emotional allergies and take inspired action to expand your tolerance of these emotions.

PART THREE
CAREER BYSTANDER TO CAREER ARCHITECT

We have now secured the two foundational layers of the Career Pivots Compass framework: time and energy management, and overcoming limitations. Let's now accelerate into the centre of the compass where you will find clarity on what comes next and the practical support to make it happen. You'll know that you can make decisions free from fear and handle people and situations that would previously have panicked and overwhelmed you.

Don't remain unconscious and passive in your career design. I hate to break it to you, but if you plan to be the most committed until you are the best, letting your work speak for itself, you will ultimately end up feeling disappointed, frustrated and bitter. This is a form of self-sabotage. It's time for a new approach that focuses on understanding and leading from your natural talents and capabilities, rather than what you have learned to be good at over time. These strengths form the new building blocks on which you can design and create a career for fulfilment using mortar made from your purpose–mission–vision. Professional positioning will get your building noticed and transition strategies will ensure that movement strengthens the structure rather than destabilises it. It's time to architect your vision of exquisite magnificence, make your greatest contribution in the world and feel purposeful and valued.

From unconscious to conscious. Passive to proactive. Self-sabotage to self-belief. Bystander to architect. This is the way to an intentional career.

6
Leadership Pathways

It was 2015. I was working as a scientific project manager at the Manchester Institute of Biotechnology and had just returned to work after my second maternity leave. In preparation for a two-day professional development residential, I completed a personality profiling test. The profile is based on the principle that we each have an underlying talent. When allowed to shine, it can improve how we work with others, help us find our ideal career pathways, and create extraordinary results.

The profile I received back was a shock because it sounded nothing like me. Analysing the report, I realised my mistake. I had answered the questions with my current job activity in mind, rather than as if I had a choice. Looking at all the other profiles revealed that I was operating at the opposite end of the spectrum to my natural talents in a classic example of 'the capability trap' – a term used in academia to describe fragile economic states,[1] but applied in the career sphere by Meredith Grey in season sixteen of *Grey's Anatomy*: 'Just because you can do something, doesn't necessarily mean that you should.'

We can all do things that do not play to our strengths, but we need to recognise that doing so will require much more of our time and energy and steal more joy. What I had been lacking in natural ability I was making up for with sheer grit, determination and hard work. No wonder I was exhausted while others around me were thriving in the same role. Are you in the capability trap? How much of your time at work are you spending on activities that light you up and give you energy rather than deplete you? You may be shocked by the percentage that you uncover.

Natural talents

Work doesn't have to feel like hard work, and if it does then something is wrong. Try using your natural talents and strengths to create a state of flow – a term coined by the author Mihaly Csikszentmihalyi.[2] Being in flow, perhaps better known as being in the zone, is a combination of having such focus that all sense of time disappears, having genuine fun, and getting great results.

The work itself may not be easy, but there will be an easeful state that comes with the task. Flow is important because, when it happens, productivity goes up, accuracy levels improve and attention levels increase. We also communicate more effectively, have more fun and feel more connected to our purpose. Our results improve dramatically.[3]

I am often asked by my clients, 'How do I speed up flow?' The secret is: instead of working on your weaknesses all the time, which is old-paradigm thinking, identify your natural talents and strengths. Find opportunities to enhance and master them through professional development. Building a team full of people with complementary talents will accelerate performance. You may also find it helpful to develop competency in skills that are not your natural talents but which you need to use in the context of your work, as well as to identify the blind spots of your natural talents and work on mitigation strategies so that they don't detract from your flow state.

Focusing on being successful and avoiding failure is the remit of the Pusher. Instead, being of value is a career driver which will benefit your self-esteem. You make a valuable contribution by shifting the focus away from yourself and how you are being perceived, and onto how you can best be of service. I use the word 'service' deliberately (and not in the derogatory sense), since our culture in the past (and still largely in the present) has dictated that our role as women is to serve. The etymology of the word 'service' is derived from the late-twelfth-century word 'serven', meaning 'to give aid'.[4] By not stepping into your natural talents, or using them to the fullest, you rob the world of the aid it needs: your gifts, you. Bringing your gifts to the world is an incredible act of service.

One great place to get started in understanding your natural talents and strengths (and therefore the value you add) is profiling tools. A vast array of them exists in the marketplace, from paid options to free quizzes. Many of the paid assessment tools have some form of basis in Carl Jung's theory of psychological types, first published in his book *Psychological Types*,[5] but a new type of report from data on natural language, genetic evidence and functional magnetic resonance imaging data is emerging from Big Five,[6] the Hogan Personality Inventory[7] and PrinciplesYou.[8]

The Myers-Briggs Type Indicator (MBTI) assessment is probably the most widely known and used personality test, with around 2.5 million people completing it annually and eighty-nine of the Fortune 100 companies using it.[9] As we saw in my own example, however, results should be interpreted with caution. Social scientist and *New York Times* bestselling author Adam Grant wrote an article in 2013 highlighting that research into the MBTI found that as many as 75% of those who took the personality test received a different result when tested again.[10]

Another paid option is Strengths Profile,[11] developed by Dr Alex Linley, who has published widely in the field of positive psychology. The report includes seven realised strengths, seven unrealised strengths, four learned behaviours and up to three weaknesses. I like the insights; in particular, those from the unrealised strengths, because sometimes things we do naturally don't feel like talents, since we have always done them.

In 2020, Strengths Profile incorporated a careers guide into the results, indicating six out of forty-three sectors which use your most realised strength, and two sectors which use your most unrealised strength. Unlike other strengths-based tools, it offers a holistic approach and a range of options, rather than labelling individuals. It accurately predicted coaching as one of the six potential sectors for my strengths, which I was impressed by.

The issue with identifying different sectors suited to your strengths is that it has the capacity to send you down a rabbit hole at a time when I want to keep you in big-picture thinking. At this stage, I recommend using a personality profile. Once you have worked through the material on career pivots in Chapter 7, then by all means consider the Strengths Profile for additional confirmation.

The mute flappy bird

Let me be clear. I urge caution in the use of these tools, especially without personal reflection and a full and comprehensive debrief with a trained professional. Having said that, they can be powerful and have an impact on understanding yourself and which roles may be a good fit. They may also help you gain excellence through targeted professional development for your talents and improved communication and team dynamics. For these reasons, I use Talent Dynamics[12] with two types of debriefs with my clients.

There's no doubt that personality profiles can come up short because of flaws in the design; however, from working with thousands of clients and deep-diving into their profiles, I have noticed another intriguing oddity. Clients who undertake a personal development journey can often feel like their initial profile isn't a good fit. Overcoming personal limitations allows them to fully embrace their natural profile.

Let me give you my own example. When I was five years old, I was cast as the snow princess in the school play. My costume was a beautiful, tall, glittery paper crown and a white dress laced with sequins. I remember in one of the rehearsals standing there in a state of fear, not knowing what they were asking me to do. I overheard one teacher say to another, 'I thought she was going to be good at this because she does all of that dancing.'

The next year, I was given the role of a bird that came on stage for ninety seconds, flapped her wings, ran around a nest of eggs then straight off the stage. I was so ashamed to be the mute flappy bird. The connections I made in my brain interpreted the message as: 'You can dance and perform, but you can't speak on any kind of platform.' This was a rule I continued to abide by until I retrained to be a coach in 2019.

I first took the Talent Dynamics personality profile back in 2015, and the result was a Trader profile, which sounded nothing like me. I had not only answered the questions against the tasks in my role at that time, rather than as if I had a choice, but I was also bound by my personal limitations. I'd had two early childhood experiences of feeling intense shame in connection with speaking in front of others, and so protection strategies included avoidance of the thing I am naturally talented at.

Although I started giving talks and keynote speeches and offering training, when I began coaching, I would still feel intense levels of anxiety before in-person events. I was no longer paralysed and avoidant, but still needed to muster a heap of courage to do the thing I loved and excelled at. It wasn't until I had fully dealt with my own tower of behaviours, and managed the underlying vulnerability, that I could fully reclaim my true Talent Dynamics Star profile.

After two years of online events during the COVID-19 pandemic, I was invited to create and facilitate a two-day future leaders forum in Washington DC. It was the first time I had been on an aeroplane, and travelled by myself, in over two years. The revelation of a positive COVID-19 case among the delegates caused a spiral of panicked thoughts.

The story in my head went something like, 'I'm going to catch Covid and have to isolate here for ten days, which is double the amount of time I've ever spent away from the children before.' I connected with and calmed the vulnerable part inside by focusing on what was within my control. I was here in Washington DC to deliver a two-day training event. I could not control catching COVID-19, beyond using the protection strategies already enforced. I went out there, delivered a transformational event and felt an overwhelming sense of fulfilment.

Had I not overcome my personal limitations, I would likely still believe my natural talents reside in a different profile. This mindset often results in going for roles based on current experience, skills and qualifications, rather than seeking out opportunities to grow into your talents, using your current environment first. This is not isolated to my own experience; I have witnessed it time and again with my clients.

The opportunity magnet

It's time for you to do some reflection. I encourage you to develop a working list of your top three talents, which I like to call your superpowers. There are a number of different ways in which you can curate this list. You can, of course, systematically review your personality profile, and decipher three top talents. You can note down times when you feel in flow and determine the talent you were using at the time. You can actively ask for, or listen out for, feedback from others, because often other people see you in a way in which you can't see yourself.

After I had delivered a workshop for the Women in Research Network at the University of York, Dr Helen Niblock, who at the time was the research development manager in physical science, sent me the following feedback: 'I was really impressed with the on-the-hoof feedback you were able to provide.'

That's when I realised thinking on my feet is one of my superpowers, along with motivating and inspiring action in others, and synthesising new ideas through exploration and discernment.

Your personality profile can point you towards your superpowers, but feedback from others will often distinguish them clearly. Start today by asking five to ten people who know you well to name your top three strengths. You may just gain invaluable insight into yourself that was previously hidden from view.

CLIENT STORY
Dr Natsuko Suwaki – the opportunity magnet

During the months following the onset of the COVID-19 lockdowns, I was invited by GSK's Women's Leadership Initiative to give nine lunch and learn sessions to over 300 members across the globe. Natsuko was one of those attendees who contacted me after the workshop series ended for one-to-one coaching support.

Natsuko started her career as a PhD researcher in cell and molecular biology, before becoming a research scientist in cancer studies. She left the bench in 2013 and joined the Global Regulatory Affairs Labelling team in the research and development function. She gained a leadership position in 2017 as the delivery manager and had been in that role for three years, yearning for a new challenge but without clarity on her next steps. Natsuko's Inner Critic was going wild, comparing her to others who seemingly had opportunities land in their laps, and she wanted the right opportunity to find her.

When Natsuko initially completed her Talent Dynamics profile, the result showed an Accumulator profile, which fitted perfectly with her role at that time. I encouraged her to remain open to discovering where she found flow and added the most value. GSK undertook a major restructure, and although there was an opening for a promotion within her team, she decided to take a sideways move into a completely new role as an operations manager in the ethics and compliance function.

On paper, according to her profile, this would have taken her wildly outside of her natural talents to a more people-focused strategy role.

I remember Natsuko saying in one of our sessions that she was concerned the work didn't feel hard enough. She was excited by it, but it was almost too easy, and this felt worrying. What she was discovering was the magic of adding value through natural talents and the feeling of ease and joy which accompanies that – a shift from an Accumulator role into her more natural and authentic 'Creator' profile.

Within a year of this move, she was promoted to governance and standards director in the legal and compliance function, enabling leaders to bring their vision and strategy to life using her superpowers of connecting the dots, creative strategy and leading through collaboration.

From the outside in, perhaps it looks like the opportunity landed in her lap; but from the inside out, I know this was only possible because she was being highly intentional in developing her natural talent skill set.

Listen to Dr Natsuko Suwaki's full podcast episode here: **https://hannahnikeroberts.com/inspiring-stories-016-natsuko-suwaki**

A role profile that fits your strengths

The great news about understanding your personality profile and natural talents and strengths is that you will be able to use these to identify roles which are a great fit for you. Before we begin, I must add a caveat: job specifications do not always accurately describe the role and what it entails. Most people only find this out when they start the job, and it's too late.

CLIENT STORY
Dr Shirin Jahandar – it's not all as it seems

Shirin was a medical advisor at a large multinational pharmaceutical company. She had been so excited to start the role because the job description had mentioned scientific liaison with clinicians and patients, which met one of her top career values. She would be able to get close and see the difference she was making first-hand.

The only trouble was, after one year it became crystal clear the liaison aspect was only a small percentage of the role: less than 5%, if she had to put a number on it. What she was spending the most time on was contracts and reports, and the writing and analysis took her away from her natural talents and strengths. She was more than capable of doing these tasks, and her manager was ecstatic with her work quality, but the result for Shirin was dissatisfaction.

She was working excessively, sacrificing evenings, weekends and family time, to complete work that fundamentally wasn't enjoyable. When you have reached stage three of the Intentional Careers journey – unsustainable – something has to change. By discovering her natural talents and flow state, Shirin was able to define roles within the organisation that were a good fit, and have powerful conversations with her manager to gain exposure to skills and projects required to make the transition.

Sometimes, when you look at a job description, you will be able to pull out specific talents or skills from the profile, but that requires a deeper level of knowledge of the profiling tools. Rather than looking at your personality profile, zoom out to the energy level.

According to Talent Dynamics, there are four different energy frequencies to pay attention to when thinking about role profiles:

1. The dynamo energy is fast-paced and innovative, and people with this type of energy are great at getting things started but not so great at completing them. They think about the big picture, strategy and ideas, and make decisions intuitively.

2. The blaze energy is all about bringing out the best in others. These people are able to lead, follow and work alongside others. They set fire to ideas by galvanising people into action.

3. In tempo energy everything gets done in the right way, at the right time. It's about being hands-on, bringing projects to fruition and providing that unique perspective.

4. The steel energy is about turning ideas into action through systems, processes and procedures; using data and insights to drive the innovation of the methods and systems.

Outlined below are the first three essential criteria listed in the key responsibilities of a real-life project manager role description. I have categorised the first essential criterion as tempo energy because it is about timelines and ensuring project completion. The second essential criterion is also tempo energy because, again, it is to do with the timings of the project. I applied steel energy to the third, due to the recommendations being made through assessing and diagnosing potential issues:

1. **Tempo energy:** Develop and maintain agreed project plans defining criteria for control and management of the project.

2. **Tempo energy:** Manage project administration, including deadlines for bi-monthly project reporting and annual milestone refreshing.

3. **Steel energy:** Identify potential issues and problems in project delivery, making recommendations to project leaders on how to address them.

When you are analysing a job specification, use a different colour for all four of the energies. Highlight each sentence in turn according to the energy required to get the task completed. By the end of the job description, you will have a clear order of preference for the energies, and once you know your profile, you will be able to see if, overall, it is a match for you. It would be unusual to find a role profile which was only one type of energy. Of course, in reality, you may find all four energies in a role, but we are looking for one or two energies in particular that dominate the profile.

When I continued to map out the role above, it resulted in an almost-even split of tempo and steel energy, which is a perfect match for someone who has the following talents: reliable, meticulous, delivers on time, organised, sees where things can go wrong, keeps the team together.

While I want you to use the process outlined above, I also encourage you to find out more about the role, and the type of day-to-day activities to expect, through informational interviews, ideally with people who are currently doing the role of interest in the place where you would like to work. Alternatively, you could interview someone with that role in your current organisation, or even a different organisation altogether.

When setting up an informational interview, ask for thirty minutes of the other person's time. Usually, people are willing to be helpful by talking about themselves and sharing their experiences. Ask them for advice, and make sure to ask questions to learn about the individual and discover more about the organisation, sector and role, including the most important question of all: 'Is there anyone else I should speak to that you can put me in contact with?' Growing your network of referrals will serve you well when you reach step number five of the Career Pivots Compass – professional positioning.

IMPLEMENT THIS

Focus on adding value by enhancing your natural talents and strengths, and explore your answers to the following questions:

- How do you define your flow state?
- What tasks have you feeling in flow?
- What tasks have you feeling out of flow?
- What comes easy to you that is hard for others?
- Ask five to ten people who know you well to name your top three strengths.
- What did you discover about yourself when you answered these questions?

7
Career Pivots

'Pivot (noun): turning point, on which some matter hinges or depends.'[1] Your next career step is not the final destination, it just needs to be slightly more aligned than the last.

Eight weeks into my third maternity leave, 'Mum calling' flashed across my phone screen. I know it sounds bizarre, but before I'd answered the phone I knew it wasn't good news. My dad was in hospital. He had suffered a huge heart attack and lost 50% of his heart function, but thankfully he was alive.

For the next week, every evening after Oscar and my younger son, Jenson, were asleep in bed, I would drive to Manchester Royal Infirmary with baby Elsie in the car seat. I would sit by my dad's bed, and we would simply talk. Those conversations seemed stripped back, more real somehow. He would shake his head with tears in his eyes in disbelief that this had happened to him. I would recite 'Peter Rabbit' to Elsie when she woke up, and Dad would just watch and listen, seemingly no longer in pain.

On the drive home every evening I would begin to ask myself big life questions: 'If I was to die today, what tangible difference would I have made in the world?' 'What is my purpose?' 'What legacy can I leave to my children and others?' It felt like my whole body was tingling with the expansiveness of possibilities. A quote by Steve Jobs played on a loop in my mind: 'Remembering that you are going to die is the best way I know to avoid the trap of thinking you have something to lose. You are already naked. There is no reason to not follow your heart.'[2]

Trust your instincts

For me, becoming a mother was an identity shift, and maternity leave afforded a period of introspection and major life re-evaluation. Usually, the epiphanies would come at two in the morning, when I couldn't easily fall back to sleep after a feed. In Chapter 2 I introduced the concept of moving away from what you want to be, and instead focusing on navigating towards a compelling vision. Making this shift also means continually upgrading, expanding and editing your identity, your 'selves'. The more you pin your career on your identity, the more you will ignore evidence if it is not aligned for you.[3]

On maternity leave, a series of synchronicities occurred. A friend invited me to a coaching workshop, and that's when my brain went from tingly to being on fire. I took all the skills I had learned as a researcher and dived deep down into the rabbit hole of coaching.

Having signed up for a coaching qualification, I emerged from my research like a snowdrop pushing its way through the earth: my whole body was viscerally saying, 'Yes, this way.' Don't just listen to logic, because your body often knows what is true for you long before the brain takes over to analyse, draw comparisons and overthink the situation. Start to reconnect with your body – and trust the wisdom it has to share with you.

On the morning of New Year's Day 2019, still on maternity leave, I registered my limited company online. Looking forwards, I was just taking the next step that was more aligned with my goals than the last, but looking back, it all makes perfect sense.

I had already been managing director of a start-up company, so I knew the first principles of how to run and manage a business. I had also already been coached for two years and had reaped the profound benefits first-hand. As a STEM woman, I knew all too well the inequitable pitfalls of trying to navigate and thrive in competitive masculine environments, and was committed to changing this paradigm. It makes me emotional writing this sentence, but having a daughter made me realise I want equity so that she and others can have a better run at things.

Steve Jobs's 2005 Stanford Commencement Address has over 40 million views on YouTube.[4] I highly recommend viewing the whole speech. My favourite excerpt says, 'You can't connect the dots looking forward, you can only connect them looking backwards, and you have to trust that the dots will somehow connect in the future.'

Do not get caught up in perfectionism. Your next step is not the final destination; it just needs to be slightly more aligned than the last. Allow that part of the process to unfold, then take the next more aligned step, until you get closer and closer to your bliss. As Joseph Campbell said, 'If you do follow your bliss, you put yourself on the kind of track that has been there all the while, waiting for you, and the life that you ought to be living is the one you are living.'[5]

No matter how much it sometimes feels like you are back at the starting line, you are not. You're always moving forwards, building on what you've learned, and you grow and change in the process. You must let go of the life your eight-year-old self, your parents and your culture planned for you. Accept that there is a new chapter, maybe even a new book, waiting for you. A new evolution of yourself.

We think we need a perfect map of the future. What we really need is a general direction which gets more refined over time: a compass.

*Using the Career Pivots Compass to create
balance, confidence and fulfilment*

The three dots

If you want to figure out 'what's next?' in your career, this is the section you have been patiently waiting for. Insights I've drawn from entrepreneurs Daniel Priestley and Glen Carlson at Dent indicate there are three components, or 'dots', to pay attention to: purpose, mission and vision. A little bit like looking up at the night sky on the ceiling of a planetarium and noticing the lines used to join the dots of constellations, you can similarly join the dots of your life purpose–mission–vision. This will give you the clarity and certainty to make decisions on your next career pivot. Remember, a pivot is a turning point on which something matters or depends. That thing is you. These dots will also serve as a continuous navigational system to keep you on track in the long-term. The Google Maps of your career.

A word of caution before we begin. Having guided thousands of women through these exercises, I have noticed that, for those of you who are already depleted, or actively in burnout, your whole system is in survival mode and these exercises most likely will not reveal your life purpose. Your Protector Controller might be trying to protect you from driving yourself further into deficit to achieve it. If you are in that place, secure foundational layer number one of the Career Pivots Compass, improving your time and energy management, until you feel more resourced. It is likely you will then be able to get definition of your purpose, mission and vision, and the inspired implementation actions, to create your next career pivot.

Do not think about this process as a tick-box exercise to be allocated a maximum of thirty minutes at 11pm on a Tuesday. Instead of constraining yourself, think of this process as a personal exploration. When you reflect, and review what you are discovering, it refines the results, giving greater depth of clarity and certainty. Essentially, you need time and space to do this properly, otherwise you will be unhappy with the results.

There's so much confusion online about purpose, mission and vision. I see organisations large and small mixing up the terminology all the time. Let me bring some distinction and discernment to each part in turn.

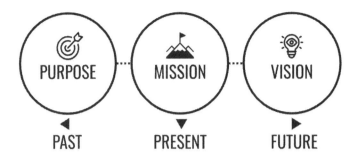

An overview of purpose-mission-vision

Purpose

You must look backwards in your life to make the connection between purpose, mission and vision, and the first dot to unfurl is life purpose. It is possible to have always known your life purpose. What would be even more miraculous is a person listening to what they know and following through on it, without wandering off course. Sometimes a major life event happens which causes a person to take an alternative path aligned to their purpose; for example, a car crash, having a baby, the death of a loved one.

For most people, purpose is something to be discovered. Your purpose lies in the past, and it is where your passions arise from. Alongside noting your passions, purpose can be deciphered from the key themes which keep replaying in your life. These may have originated from positive or negative experiences, but they shaped and continue to guide you.

I encourage you to uncover your life purpose themes by mapping out a timeline of your life with high and low points. Start as early in your life as you can, noting down details for each memory. Then, look for the life purpose themes by distilling your timeline into the lessons learned and how they relate back to your career. You will most likely also see some of your talents represented here. For example, one of my life themes is to motivate and inspire. This also happens to be a primary strength of my Talent Dynamics personality profile. The result of understanding your purpose is being able to answer the question, 'What drives you to get out of bed every morning and show up for work?'

Mission

The next dot in our series is the mission. Your mission is in the present, and it is where you can find personal power, because you have the power to change what you do and the way in which you express it in the world. Mission is the specific what-you-are-up-to in the world. My greatest wish for you is that your mission is a place for self-expression, through both love and play. If work feels like hard work, then we are doing it wrong. If you are working right now, your current mission is the current role you are doing, whether you like it or not. You self-express your mission through your natural talents and career values. Mission is powerful because you can change it at any time by undergoing the Career Pivots process.

There is your personal mission, and there is also the mission of the organisation within which you work. What you are looking for is a substantial overlap between the two, like the beautiful concentric circles in a Venn diagram. I even created my own organisation so that I could have complete overlap between my personal and workplace missions. Do not get disheartened if you do not currently have any overlap because you have just discovered the potential for a career pivot.

Equally, career is not the only place you can find mission overlap. Back in 2019, I volunteered for over a year as the UK and Ireland pod co-ordinator for 500 Women Scientists, whose mission is 'to serve society by making science open, inclusive, and accessible by fighting racism, patriarchy, and oppressive societal norms'.[6] If you are currently struggling to express your mission through your career, then see if it could be enhanced by contribution through volunteer roles.

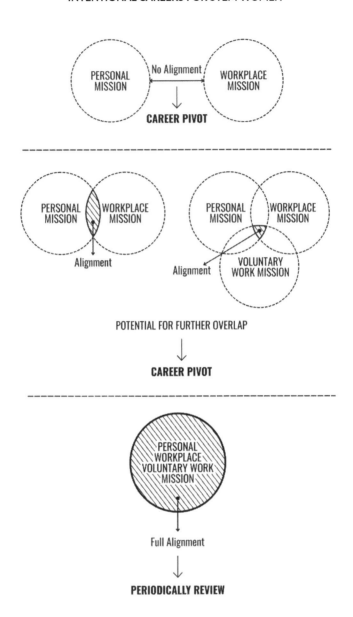

*Determining career pivots from personal,
workplace and volunteer missions*

CLIENT STORY
Dr Jane Scanlon – finding joy after a shock redundancy

When I first started working with Dr Jane Scanlon, she was a senior scientist and felt ready to take the next step in her career. We mapped out her values, creating a list of criteria she needs to be in place to feel happy and fulfilled at work. Jane realised one of her fundamental career values was to have a great collaborative team dynamic. She isn't the sort of person who gets a piece of information like that and does nothing with it. She was quickly in action, searching for her next career pivot, and took a risk joining a new start-up. Within a matter of weeks, the company was making redundancies and she was to be included.

Jane impressed me with the resilience she showed handling this news. She quickly lined up a number of interviews, and even turned down one job offer, because she was able to use our coaching assessment criteria to make an informed choice. As a result, she is now working three days a week at Sentinel Oncology, which feels fully aligned to her vision. In addition, she is volunteering for a charity and a social enterprise. When she gave me this news, I could see the joy lighting up her face as she described the immense pleasure she gained through volunteering and being able to serve by solving meaningful problems.

Vision

Your vision holds the key to making navigational decisions around career pivots. Vision is out there in the future. It's the thing that you care about changing the most in the world. One of the frameworks I love using for vision is The 17 Global Goals for Sustainable Development. Visit **https://sdgs.un.org/goals** for further details.

Pick one goal for your head. Which goal makes the most sense for you to choose based on your education and work experience so far? Pick one goal for your heart. Which goal do you care about the most? Yes, you can pick more than one for the heart but please be discerning about your choices so that you don't end up with too many competing directions.

What do you see, hear or feel at the intersection between your chosen goals? This is your vision, and it can start to inform the organisations and sectors in which you might want to work. Go ahead and create a gold list, a top ten list of organisations that fit your vision.

It is unlikely that your vision will be unique. I would be worried if it was. You will most likely have a vision that other people are already trying to create meaningful solutions around, which is exciting because you have options for what type of organisations you might be most suited to: for example, large, medium, small or micro-organisations; start-ups, charities, not-for-profits; freelancer or entrepreneur. Even as an entrepreneur, I can partner with other organisations that are in alignment with my vision. I do not want to be on a desert island working on equity all by myself. I love being in close contact with an archipelago of islands and continue to seek opportunities to further collaborate on these efforts.

The three major career pivots

Once you have successfully mapped out your purpose–mission–vision, it is time to decipher your next career pivot. There are three possible career pivots and you may meet the requirements for one, two or all three. These pivots may happen in one go, or in a series of strategic moves.

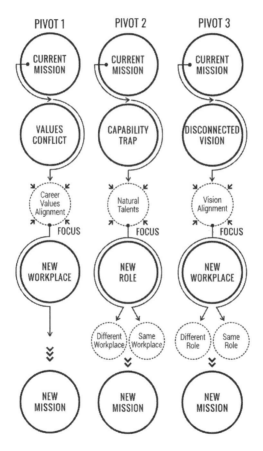

The three career pivots

Pivot number one: A values conflict

This is when you are experiencing a conflict between your values and the values of the organisation in which you work. For example, if you value balance but the unwritten rules of the organisation dictate working evenings and weekends as standard, you have a values conflict. If you value integrity but have been asked to do something illegal or outside of your integrity, you have a values conflict. Value equity but your organisation's fancy DEI statements are not implemented in practice? Values conflict.

Your values may differ from the ones highlighted above, but you get the point. If you are experiencing this type of conflict, then your focus needs to be on the alignment of your career values. I am a big advocate of making the current situation as good as it can be. Get clear on those career values (the criteria you need to feel happy and fulfilled at work) and have conversations with your manager about how you can improve your career values scores to get more of what you want. Use those values as a blueprint for gaining fulfilment and assessing opportunities.

Some of the examples above, though, require workplace culture shifts. I wholeheartedly back new structures, policies and procedures to achieve this, such as access to high-quality, affordable childcare as a vital social infrastructure. For this to happen, we need a shift in workplace cultures and to look at the implicit biases that infiltrate the cultural soup we swim in. To do those things, we need individuals to feel resourced enough to lobby the leadership teams for change.

Those critical structural and policy changes rarely come from top-down leadership; they happen from the bottom up. Think of the government-wide policy introduced in May 2021 to ensure retailers of any size charge a minimum of ten pence for single-use carrier bags in England.[7] This policy does change behaviour. If I forget my bag for life, I'm the one that balances everything under my chin and arms rather than buying yet another plastic bag. How about you?

It was the Climate Change Act 2008 and the Climate Change (Scotland) Act 2009 that provided the legislative framework for the single-use carrier bag charge,[8] resulting in a reduction of over 97% in the number of carrier bags since the charge was introduced.[9] The 2008 Climate Change Bill was preceded by a Private Members' bill of the same name,[10] drafted by Friends of the Earth and brought before Parliament on 7 April 2005.[11]

What appears to be a top-down government policy actually originates from a small group of committed people at Friends of the Earth. If you are ever feeling powerless to change the system, please remember your personal agency, or as Margaret Mead remarks, 'Never doubt that a small group of thoughtful, committed citizens can change the world; indeed, it's the only thing that ever has.'[12]

When thousands of thoughtful, committed people come together, movements can magically materialise. For example, women's rights movements, such as the formation of the National Society for Women's Suffrage in 1872, to fight for women's right to vote in the UK, and later the more influential National Union of Women's Suffrage Societies, which grew to 50,000 members by 1913.[13]

One of two things could happen if you start to stand up for your values at work. Either the workplace embraces you, and welcomes your insights and enthusiasm for change, in which case there may be hope for staying within the organisation and driving or influencing the outcomes, or your requests are not acknowledged or welcomed. The latter is a sure-fire sign to move beyond your current organisation, using your career values as the blueprint, to ensure your next role and place of work meet your standards for fulfilment.

PIVOT 1

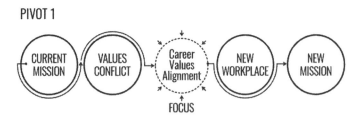

Career pivot 1: Values conflict

Pivot number two: The capability trap

I went into detail about how to recognise if you are in the capability trap in Chapter 6. Please revisit this content if you are unsure about what it means.

You are in the capability trap if you are working in a role that is not a fit for your natural talents and strengths. Start by recognising and using your strengths in your current role. Praise yourself every time you add your unique value. You may need to become skilled at reclaiming your boundaries and delegating the things that take you out of flow to start with. Assuming there is someone to delegate to, of course; I know this will not be an option for everyone. When you are good at this, you will also need to learn how to say no or delegate the things you love to do, as you won't have enough time for everything, even if it is a talent for you.

If you are not able to develop your role to enhance your natural talents, then you will need a new role that does. The new role can be in either the same organisation, if you feel aligned with the organisational vision, or a new organisation that provides a crossover with your own vision. As a result of shifting roles, you will be living a new mission.

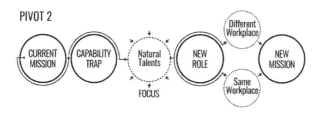

Career pivot 2: The capability trap

Pivot number three: A disconnected vision

Perhaps you have been lured into being shaped and moulded to fit someone else's vision. You may have bought into it because of their infectious enthusiasm, but ultimately, their vision is not what you care about most in the world. Maybe you are working unsustainably to fulfil their vision. If this is the case, ask yourself why. What does it give you? Be prepared, you might not like the answer as you hold up the mirror to your own behaviours and actions, and remember: the reason I ask you to do this is to form awareness, to prime you for choice and change.

If you are experiencing a disconnected vision with your organisation, you will ultimately need to move to a new workplace. This can be in the same type of role, or a different role if you are also experiencing the capability trap. Career pivots may happen in a series of strategic moves, or one big leap that fulfils all the changes required at that moment. Neither way is right or wrong, good or bad; it all comes down to what opportunities you can create with this information – a strategy I will outline in Chapter 8.

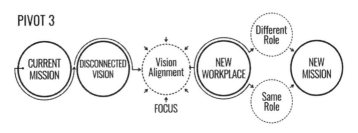

Career pivot 3: Disconnected vision

CLIENT STORY
Dr Judith Simon – coalescence of career pivots

I started working with Judith during her transition from postdoc to becoming a senior regulatory scientist in the field of medical writing at RQM+. Her career value of work–life balance was in conflict in academia, as well as in the role profile itself, dropping her into the capability trap.

We had previously analysed her Talent Dynamics profile and discovered she was a Supporter profile. Judith felt this profile accurately described her personality and talents: someone who turns ideas into action by bringing out the best in other people.

The role she had taken as a senior regulatory scientist matched her learned skills of being analytical and detail-orientated, but it was not a 100% match for her natural talents. In one session she was struggling to adapt to being isolated when working from home, because of her need for connection with others. She devised a plan to meet her basic need for connection, which included taking lunch breaks to meet with friends, and actively planning glimmer moments of connection into her daily routine.

These are moments of connection with oneself, the environment, or others, which can be completed in under a minute. Some of my favourites include closing my eyes for a quick meditation (you can find some great examples on the Insight Timer app), scanning my attention down my whole body, noticing the breeze on my face, going outside and feeling my feet grounded on the earth, and sending a message of gratitude to my husband or a friend – a fantastic use for technology if you can avoid the lure of those red notifications. Don't forget to turn your phone off afterwards, put it in another room, or use a focus timer app such as Forest, Pomodor, Session or Toggl Track.

Six months after Judith started, an internal job was advertised for a capability manager role within a hub of people supporting the development of others. For Judith it was an amazing opportunity to find something internal at the organisation that matched her natural talents and would help develop those skills to the level of mastery. She had previously believed she would need to change organisations to find a role that was a good fit.

Although unsuccessful at the interview, she was not disheartened, because being clear and vocal about what she wanted within the organisation opened up conversations about how to progress towards this new goal. She took on more people-focused tasks and management in her current role and is taking steps to develop these skills through professional training opportunities.

 Listen to Dr Judith Simon's full podcast episode at https://hannahnikeroberts.com/inspiring-stories-022-dr-judith-simon.

IMPLEMENT THIS

- Go to the website of your current organisation. Can you find their mission?

- How much resonance or dissonance do you feel with this mission? Give it a score between +10 and −10.

- Are you using your natural talents more than 80% of the time in your role?

- Do you have a score of more than 8 out of 10 for your top five career values?

- Discover your current mission by completing this sentence: I help [insert stakeholders impacted by your work] achieve [insert big outcome] by [how do you achieve those results].

- Visit https://sdgs.un.org/goals. Pick one goal for your head and one for your heart. What do you see, hear or feel at the intersection between these goals?

- Find five target organisations that work within the realm of the intersection you have described.

8
Personal Branding

The exercises in Chapter 7 helped you connect the 'dots' between your purpose, mission and vision to gain clarity on the type of pivots you are currently undertaking. Each pivot you take will move you closer and closer to your fulfilment bliss. When you have connected your dots, you will not just experience fulfilment, you'll be vital. Not only will you feel an internal shift of activation and energy, but you'll also feel an external and noticeable shift. People who have achieved this shine and have a glint in their eye which says, 'I'm up to something special in the world.' They are the people who don't wait for opportunities – they create them.

This chapter will outline the actionable steps you can take to embrace those new opportunities by using online networking strategies, because your success undoubtedly depends on your ability to influence. This does not mean that you suddenly need to become an Instagram or TikTok influencer, unless that is something that appeals to you. I'm talking about having a professional social media network, and applying a specific strategy, to create the next opportunity you are looking for.

According to the most recent Conference Board Annual Survey, hiring talent remains the number one concern of CEOs. It's also the top concern of the entire executive suite.[1] PwC's twenty-sixth annual CEO survey reports chief executives view talent, skills and technology as the biggest threats to their business, with 22% of UK CEOs stating their business will not be viable in a decade unless they change course.[2]

The top five channels for quality hires in order of preference are: employee referrals, third-party websites or online job boards, social or professional networks, third-party recruiters or staffing firms, and internal hires.[3] All five of those channels are in some way accessible using LinkedIn. This is why I strongly recommend you apply the learning here to that platform, although everything I'm about to guide you through will work on other social media platforms too (and there will of course be platform-specific nuances that are not covered).

Making the shift to online networking also means creating a personal brand. The benefits of self-promotion are vast, and include taking control of how you are perceived by others and helping others to understand your value and contribution. Think of your personal brand as the thing you want to be known for, your thought leadership, which, put simply, is having an opinion on something that matters to you.

Virgin is a well-established household name which has been around since the 1970s. At the time of writing, Virgin has 250,000 followers on Twitter.[4] Richard Branson, the founder, has 12.6 million followers.[5] Business branding is important, but people connect with people, so you can't hide behind your organisation, you need to have your own personal brand.

Show up professionally online

Whenever I run workshops and courses on professional online networking, the most common barriers I hear are not knowing how impactful online tools really are, not knowing what to say, and not wanting to sound arrogant. No one wants to lose focus and waste time being sucked into consuming social media, or to leave a permanent trace, without the evidence it produces tangible results.

We have all seen examples of overt bragging and humblebragging online, and we can smell both a mile off. Without exercising the ability to sell themselves, individuals are likely to languish behind their self-promoting peers. Self-promotion is like a muscle that needs flexing to get stronger over time. Remember that it's not bragging if it's a fact.[6]

There are three strategies you can use to ensure you show up online purposefully. Remember that whichever strategy you use, it is just for now, not forever. For example, if your strategy for now is seeking a new job opportunity and then you get hired, you don't continue with the job opportunity strategy, you shift into a different one. Please choose from the following:

1. Strategy number one is job opportunities. Only pick this strategy if you need a new job opportunity in the next six months, and you are clear on what you are looking for. If you don't have clarity yet, don't worry, keep working on your purpose–mission–vision until it does become clear, and pick one of the other strategies for now.

2. Strategy number two is collaborations, partnerships or sales. Pick this strategy if you want to seek collaborations with others in your given area of expertise, or with those that align to a particular vision. You might need to develop partnerships with other people in your role in organisations of interest. If you are a freelancer, entrepreneur, or you work in sales and marketing, you may use your professional network to enhance sales.

3. Strategy number three is increasing the visibility for the work you currently do, either internally in the organisation or through engaging with other stakeholders who are impacted by your work.

By default, strategies one and two also bring increased visibility, but the purpose behind the visibility is different. If you are still unclear on your next career pivot, then use this strategy for now until you have clarity.

Now apply your strategy lens to everything that is covered in the next sections so that you can create the opportunity you are looking for.

A dusty old CV

On 1 January 2019, I incorporated my company and had 465 connections on LinkedIn. I used LinkedIn like a dusty old CV. The only time I would log in or update it was when going for a new job opportunity. How wrong I was to approach it in this way. Over the course of the next six months, I grew my network from 465 to about 9,000, and by the start of 2023 I had over 25,000 connections.

Now, it's not the size of the network that is important at the beginning; it is the laser vision focus: seeing every person in your network as your ideal manager, collaborator, partner, client or stakeholder; the person you want to connect and network with, over and over again.

For example, if you picked strategy number one, job opportunities, then your ideal person will be your next manager, or recruiters who can hire you into

those positions. Recruiters and talent acquisition partners are the perfect group of people to connect with
because they have large, targeted networks. If you are
contacted by a recruiter and the position is of interest to you, then this is also a great piece of data to
show that your profile is working for you rather than
against you. If a recruiter contacts you about a role
you would have been suitable for five years ago, your
profile is well overdue an overhaul.

Once you have the focus sorted, it is then about
increasing the volume of that specified network. Having a large and targeted network will future-proof
your career. You may also receive an influx of other
opportunities that are not even conceivable at this
moment in time. I have been asked to write paid articles, featured on panels and podcasts, requested as a
keynote speaker at events, and even headhunted for
job offers. You will notice an increase in additional
inbound enquiries and opportunities too.

If you are already thinking, 'I don't want to grow
my professional network, it's already hard for me to
keep up with notifications as it is', please read this section with a beginner's mind. I aim for you to reduce
your time spent on social media, not increase it, by
using three clearly defined actions. If the COVID-19
pandemic has taught us anything, it is just how important making the shift to using online resources is. It is
usually only when we need our networks the most
that we realise how much they have been neglected
and deprioritised.

Elevate your LinkedIn profile

I am going to share with you three elegant strategies you can use in under fifteen minutes to expand your network, increase interconnectivity and make you more visible. One of the main drains on your time and energy is consuming social media, so whenever you go on the platform, resist the temptation to do so. Take these three steps, and if you have time left over to consume, go ahead. Make sure you set a timer though.

Step One: Expand your network by ten relevant people a day

Go to the search bar and type in your search term for your ideal person. This could be their job title, a qualification or a sector-specific word. Once you have hit the search button, select 'People', click '2nd', for second-degree connections. Drill down by location or organisation, if this is relevant to your search, and pick ten people to connect with. When you have narrowed your list of second-degree contacts, if you are on your phone simply click the plus button, or alternatively you may see a person icon with a plus button to click. If you are using a PC, the two options you can click are 'Connect' or 'Follow', depending on how the person has set up their profile.

Of course, not everyone will accept your connection request and that's OK too, in the same way as when you get a connection request you perform a few checks first. Do you have anyone in common? Do they have a small number of connections? If you don't personally know someone and they have seven connections, why are they trying to connect with you? Does it make sense to have this person in your network? It needs to make sense if you have not met them in person. The people you are trying to connect with are also doing similar checks on you. Don't forget to set your settings to public to make this process easier. If you have your settings switched to private, other people won't see your photo or headline.

Step Two: Comment on five posts

After you have connected with ten relevant people, it is time to increase the dynamism and interconnectivity of your network by commenting on five posts. It's not enough to just like or emoji a post; when you comment on a post you become visible, and people will see your name, picture and your LinkedIn headline. If your headline makes sense, your ideal people will click through to read more about you. My clients often say to me, 'I saw your comment on my colleague's post and I clicked through to your profile, and now I'm talking to you.' I want you to have inbound experiences just like this too.

There are two main reasons why you would comment on a post. The first is to be a supportive voice in your network. Which posts can you celebrate?

Please use your own authentic way of doing this. The second reason is to add your unique value. Which posts are about subjects you are an expert on and can add value to in some way? Can you ask a question and contribute to the discussion?

If you have not been active on LinkedIn, then your home feed may not be showing relevant posts. You need to teach LinkedIn's algorithm what you want to see more of. To do this, search again using a keyword for your topic area. For example, I might type in 'imposter syndrome'. Search for posts to comment on, and potentially relevant people to connect with too. If you check out your analytics dashboard, you will see if the strategy is working by the number of people who are viewing your profile.

Step Three: Share one piece of content

You have expanded your network by ten relevant people, and increased the interconnectivity of your network by commenting on five posts. What next? I suggest being consistent with these two actions first, before adding in the final strategy. LinkedIn has over 760 million users, of which 310 million are active at least once a month, but only 1% of those are posting content.[7] Anything you do post will be super visible and, from my own experience, content hangs around longer on the LinkedIn platform.

Thought leadership increases your strategic visibility and, as Denise Brosseau writes in *Ready to be a*

Thought Leader? How to increase your influence, impact and success, it is the best career insurance around.[8] You don't want to be solely reliant on your manager to champion you in the workplace. They may leave, your organisation could merge or be sold, technology may evolve, or the economy may fall into a recession. Whatever the reason, don't let the disappearance of your champion negatively shape your long-term career aspirations. Thought leaders can always access their dynamic network, and are highly sought after for new opportunities.

The easiest way to get started with the final strategy of sharing one piece of content is to share something that already exists, like an article written by someone else. Don't just share the article though, offer your opinion on it, or a quote from the text. This sets in motion the process of developing your thought leadership.

Content is also a way to reach multiple different types of people in your network. My profile is aligned with individual STEM women, and lots of my content is created with them in mind. I also do a lot of keynote speaking, and run workshops in particular for women's networks, so I will post content about me doing these events to promote this element of my business. In the same way, you may have multiple stakeholders. Pick the most important one and align your profile to them, and then use content to reach your other stakeholders.

Think about what level of frequency you commit to these actions, because it is consistency of action that matters here. Implementing these actions once is great, but being consistent over a long period of time is what creates results. Make the pledge today. Will it be five times a week, three times a week or once a week? Anything less than once a week will not yield the results you are looking for.

Impact statements

Even if you are not ready to apply for new roles or go for interviews just yet, take the time to review the final parts of this section before you reach Chapter 10, Propelling Strategies. Reading this part now will give you a baseline understanding which you can refer to in more detail when the time is right. Because people are so focused on naming skills from job adverts in their CVs and cover letters, they forget to add context by listing the results obtained by the skill set acquired. If you want to stand out and get invited to interview or headhunted, then you need to create a series of impact statements which you can highlight on your CV and cover letter, as well as including them under 'Experience' on your LinkedIn profile: skill/talent + context + result = impact statement.

Here are two examples of using a skill or natural talent to create a context-driven, quantifiable impact statement. Reread them without the quantifiable information, and you will quickly understand why this part makes all the difference:

'I have the ability to think on my feet, which I demonstrated by facilitating nine online lunch and learn webinars for 300+ staff in GSK's Global Women's Leadership Initiative, responding to on-the-go live audience questions and providing coaching demos.'

'I have a natural talent for motivating and inspiring people into action. I have facilitated A Guide to Virtual Networking workshops to over 1,000 people, and 100% of participants who responded to the follow-up survey reported making changes to their LinkedIn profile that have positively improved their social selling index score.'

To give you some inspiration, here are a range of impact statements created by my clients in the Career Design Mastermind programme:

- I am an effective communicator, as demonstrated by co-ordinating twenty-plus cross-functional and international subject matter experts to collaborate on pass rate improvement goals for the product pipeline, raising the first-time pass rate by over 25% within six months to meet strategic goals, and saving over £1 million.

- I am efficient and reliable when under pressure, as demonstrated by managing high demand and fast turnaround on bespoke manufacture, resulting in successful orders from twenty-one customers and revenue of £2.5 million since 2021, with a complaint rate of less than 1%.

- I am highly analytical, applying the use of data to decision-making, as demonstrated by troubleshooting batch failures and increasing manufacturing controls, resulting in pass rate improvements above 90%.

- I can work to extremely strict timescales and in exacting detail, which I demonstrated by co-ordinating the transport of scientific equipment worth over £500,000 from twelve institutes in the UK to Beijing, China, and India. Customs and logistical documents had to be completed to meet freight shipping deadlines to allow for research on projects with budgets totalling over £5 million to be carried out. As part of this process, I developed new standard forms and interconnected documents to improve efficiency and reduce errors when shipping equipment across multiple institutes, which are now used exclusively by our external logistics provider.

- I am skilled in resource management, which I demonstrated by developing a new gas chromatography instrument, and improving the existing research methodologies, to reduce analysis time by 50% and consumable usage by 30%.

- I am highly skilled in project and programme management, which I have demonstrated by managing up to five projects concurrently at any one time, where I was called upon to organise resources, chair meetings, accurately record and monitor progress, risk, and actions effectively. I communicated with internal and external experts and lay colleagues to produce white papers upon project completion for senior university leaders, including the chief operating officer, deans and vice-chancellor.

- I designed, implemented and managed fifteen individual and collaborative interdisciplinary research projects over eight years, across five countries, resulting in twelve papers, three of which were first-author.

- I delivered state-of-the-art and evidence-based content through workshops, training and courses to over 300 people, of whom 80% stated they felt better able to tackle problems going forward.

IMPLEMENT THIS

- Review your transferable skills and personality profile results. Create one impact statement for each work or education experience, and add them all as highlighted skills to your LinkedIn profile, CV and the second paragraph of your cover letter. Remember: skill/talent + context + result = impact statement.

- Make sure you are consistent in your approach, and go out there and develop your thought leadership on what truly matters to you.

- Before you consume any social media, take each of these three actions in under fifteen minutes to future-proof your career, so that you have the network available to you when you need it the most: expand your network by reaching out to ten relevant people; increase your interconnectivity by commenting on five posts; get visible by sharing a post with your opinion (thought leadership).

- The key to converting your network into ideal opportunities is consistency. Pick a frequency of action and time of day, and think through how you will achieve that action. For example, 'I commit to taking these three actions Mon–Fri between 9am and 9.15am by blocking out my calendar and setting a phone alarm.' Warning: do not consume any social media before you take these actions, otherwise you will never achieve the results you are looking for.

9
Professional Positioning

What is the purpose of a CV? When I ask this question, people usually look a bit perplexed. 'To showcase my skills and qualifications' or 'to prove I can do the job' is the typical response. We need to flip these assumptions and rethink our approach. On average, only 11% of CVs sent with job applications receive a callback.[1] The purpose of a CV is to get you to the next stage in the process, which is typically the first interview. It doesn't matter if you are qualified, or if you have the right skills or desire for the job; if you can't get past the CV-screening phase, unfortunately, none of those matter.

Applicant tracking systems (ATS) are pieces of software used by companies to assist with HR, recruitment and hiring processes. According to Jobscan, 99% of Fortune 500 companies use ATS, and a growing number of small and medium-sized businesses are adopting the software too.[2] In 2021, Accenture and Harvard Business School published the report, *Hidden Workers: Untapped talent*, which stated that 90% of companies use technology to rank and filter candidates.[3] This does not mean 90% of CVs are rejected by ATS, a point often misrepresented in the media.[4] ATS screen out qualified applications in 88% of companies because they don't match the search terms the ATS has been asked to track from the job advertisement. Rather than an ATS problem, we can think of this issue as not tailoring your CV to the job role.

The Accenture and Harvard Business School report also concluded that ATS screening is not only about matching keywords between the job advert and your CV; more than 50% of companies screened out applicants because they had a gap of six months or more on their CV.

Work gaps typically fall under these five main categories:

1. Caring for sick family members

2. Attending to personal health issues

3. Receiving additional training/education

4. Raising a family

5. Other reasons

There has always been a stigma associated with employment gaps. As I discussed earlier in Chapter 3, many of my clients were told to make it look like maternity leave never happened on their CV, implying they should use maternity leave to complete work tasks such as writing papers and applying for grants. The charity Pregnant Then Screwed even took the UK government to court over the Self-employed Income Support Scheme, which likened maternity leave to a work sabbatical.[5] The Treasury made payments to the self-employed based on average profits earned between 2016 and 2019, meaning an estimated 75,000 women who took maternity leave during that period would lose out on a proportion of the money. If you have a job, you're designated employed when on maternity, paternity, adoption, disability or sick leave; therefore you do not necessarily have to disclose the leave on your CV, it can simply be included within your dates of employment. Disclosing your employment gap, however, does provide an opportunity to describe how your career, or productivity, may have been impacted.

This is important because applicants with work gaps have a 45% lower chance of securing job interviews. In 2019, researchers sent CVs showing various work gaps to 36,000+ job openings.[6] Interview chances significantly decreased for applicants with gaps of three or more years. Applicants who provided a reason for their work gap received close to 60% more interviews. Also worth noting is that among applicants who provided a reason for their work gap, those who said they received additional training or education in that time ended up with the highest interview rate.

CV structure

As you can imagine, I have seen the full range of CV lengths, from one-pagers to a forty-three-page document with a contents section. Single-page CVs are seen as the latest trend, particularly when applying for a role within a start-up. On the other hand, having a longer CV provides more space to detail work experience and accomplishments. Rather than basing my conclusions on personal preference, I prefer empirical evidence. Research by ResumeGo found that recruiters are 2.3 times more likely to prefer two-page CVs. They scored two-page CVs 21% higher and spent twice as much time reading them.[7]

With ever-growing applicant numbers, CV formatting has real impact. The human brain is hardwired to look for shortcuts and make information easier to digest. You can make this process easier still by providing clear headings and easy-to-read fonts, such as Arial or Calibri in size 11 or 12 point.

You must of course tailor your CV to every job application. There's no getting around this piece of work. A master CV is useful to have for reference, but it will not serve you well to send it out without editing it for the specific job role and specification you are applying for. Start by analysing the job description. Make a note of the top five skills and three specific keywords that need to feature in your CV to help it fly effortlessly through the ATS. For example, if the job advert says 'experience with clinical trials' is essential, make sure you use the word 'clinical trials' in your CV. Don't paraphrase or use synonyms. With those keywords in mind, here are the must-have sections for your CV.

Name, professional title and contact details

The title of your CV is not Curriculum Vitae, it is your name – including your professional title if you have one. If you use Dr as your title, it is not necessary to add the letters PhD after your name, just pick one or the other. Add your email address and feature your LinkedIn profile underneath. Think carefully about the email address you use, because 89% of HR professionals and recruitment consultants are deterred from shortlisting a candidate with an unprofessional email address.[8] Recruiters do check your online professional presence, so make sure you regularly update your LinkedIn profile details.

Example:

- Hannah Roberts, PhD, MChem (Hons)
- hannah@hannahnikeroberts.com
- www.linkedin.com/in/hannahrobertscoaching

Highlights

The highlights section should feature three key highlights of your career that are relevant to the role as bullet points.

Example:

- Host of the five-star, top ten UK podcast, Women in STEM Career and Confidence, which has received over 50,000 downloads.

Relevant experience

This is the section where you can make some of the biggest gains, and which sets you apart from all the other candidates. Most CVs provide the dates of employment, company name and role title, followed by a summary of the role. When describing the role, people often focus on what they did rather than the impact they created. The impact statement is where you align your key skills and attributes to the key-words you found in the role specification. Take a key skill, add the context in which you have used that skill, and a quantifiable outcome.

Example:

Jan 2019–present: Managing director, Breakthrough Talent & Skills Limited

Head coach and trainer, supporting STEM women to figure out 'what's next?' in their careers and the strategy to make it happen; coaching, training, speaking

Key skill: I have the ability to think on my feet, which I demonstrated by facilitating live coaching demonstrations on nine online lunch and learn webinars for GSK's Global Women's Leadership Initiative to 300+ women – www.gsk.com/en-gb/home.

Professional licences

Include this section only if you hold professional licences that are relevant to the role. It should include the name of the licence, the name of the organisation, and the date awarded.

Example:

Professional Certified Coach, International Coaching Federation, 2021

Education

It is not necessary to include qualifications you obtained prior to your degree. Include qualification from degree onwards.

Example:

MChem (Hons) in Chemistry 1st class (2000–2004)
PhD in Chemistry (2008–2011)

Volunteer experience

Adding relevant volunteer experience is a fantastic way to demonstrate your skills and values. For example, you may have developed leadership or team management skills in the volunteer context before you had the opportunity in the professional sphere. You can outline the roles in a similar way to the work experience section.

Example:

June 2019–Sept 2021: UK and Ireland 500 Women Scientists Regional Pod Co-ordinator

500 Women Scientists serve society by making science open, inclusive and accessible: https:// 500womenscientists.org. I lead the UK and Ireland pod region and support pod leaders to maintain and grow active communities. I gift 10% of my company profits annually.

References

Include two referees you are happy to be contacted. Leave this section off if you do not wish referees to be contacted before you have been offered the role.

Example:

Joe Bloggs | Joe.bloggs@emailprovider.com

Overcoming barriers

To give yourself the maximum chance of progressing to the next stage, minimise unconscious biases by not including a headshot, marital status, age or date of birth.

All too often I hear people saying, 'I don't have everything that is listed on the essential criteria list. I need to get a qualification, or to take a course before I can apply.' Far too often, people let their Inner Critics make comparisons, and the negative self-talk prevents them from trying.

You've probably heard the following statistic: men apply for a job when they meet only 60% of the essential criteria, whereas women apply only if they meet 100%. The finding comes from a Hewlett Packard internal report, and has been widely quoted in articles, usually invoked as evidence that women need more confidence.[9]

The real barrier to applying often isn't lack of confidence; the most common response was, 'I didn't think they would hire me since I didn't meet the criteria and I didn't want to waste my time and energy.'

During my podcast interview with award-winning DEI expert Siwan Smith, Siwan gave an amazing piece of advice about how to view the essential criteria of job adverts: 'If you meet all of the essential criteria then you can do the job already, there's no growth available to you in that role.' This is the tactic that has allowed Siwan to rise so quickly. She looks strategically at the essential criteria for skills to develop and grow. She says, 'If one of the essential criteria is having led a team of people, and you haven't done that before, be upfront about that being one of the main reasons you want to apply for the role.'

 You can listen to Siwan Smith's podcast episode here: **https://hannahnikeroberts.com/inspiring-stories-007-siwan-smith**.

Three-part cover letter

In 2021, a study by ResumeLab showed that 83% of hiring managers said cover letters were important in their hiring decision. They gave preference to candidates who submitted them even if it wasn't required, and 63% of hiring managers said they read the cover letter, with more than half of those saying they read it after reviewing the CV and seeing if the candidate was qualified.[10]

A cover letter should be a maximum of one page, use the standard business layout of three paragraphs, and be addressed to the correct person: the person who would be your manager if you were to get the job. Use the company's HR team, LinkedIn searches and your personal contacts to find the hiring manager's name.

Outlined below is the structure of the three paragraphs. Informational interviews are invaluable here for answering these questions, particularly those in paragraph three.

1. Referral and elevator pitch

   - Mention who referred you to the advert and the role you are applying for in the first sentence.

   - Answer the question, 'Why do you want the role?'

2. Why are you a match for the role?

   - State your ethos towards the role.

   - Include two to three bullet point impact statements that prove you have the skills to carry out the role.

3. Why are you a match for the organisation?

   - Explain why you want to work at that particular organisation.

   - Give examples of how you align with their organisational vision and values.

   - Outline what success looks like for someone in that role. This is your personal vision for the role.

Throughout history, people have been dependent on technology. Of course, the technology of each era might not have the same shape and size as today. I can't mention optimising your LinkedIn profile, writing your CV or crafting a cover letter without introducing the rise of artificial intelligence (AI), such as ChatGPT (developed by Open AI),[11] Google Bard[12] and MS Bing[13] – to name just a few. From now on you will be either powered by AI to create value as an important and highly sought-after technical skill, or left behind and diminished by the AI technological revolution.

In ChatGPT you can use the prompt, 'Write my cover letter for the [insert the job role you are applying for] at [insert the name of the organisation you are applying to] in a conversational tone, using the role specification and my CV below as a reference.' Type 'shift + enter' to create a new line. From here you can paste the additional documentation. When you get your result, save it and ask ChatGPT to generate two more versions. Pull together what you like from each version.[14]

If you are going to use AI, be aware of its limitations.[15] Only you can personalise the information. Only you know how you have demonstrated specific highlighted skills, what your vision for the role is and how you personally fit with the organisation's mission, vision and values. What you *can* currently rely on AI for is to do the heavy lifting by creating a first draft. Use other AI technology, such as the Hemingway App, to make your writing grammatically correct and clear.

Interview strategy

In December 2022, job interview statistics were released by StandOutCV. The most cited reason an applicant would fail a job interview was not an inability to demonstrate technical ability, enthusiasm or rapport; it was a fundamental lack of understanding of the role or company mission. Please pay attention to doing the research required for the interview questions.[16]

There are six main types of interview questions.

Basic interview questions

Basic interview questions are where you will need to be able to answer the question, 'Tell me about yourself and why you have applied for this role.' You need a winning introduction that condenses your qualifications and work experience in a couple of sentences.

For example, my winning introduction is, 'Hello, I'm Hannah. I have a degree, master's, PhD and post-doc in chemistry. I spent eight years managing large multimillion-pound projects between academia and industry, and commercialising that research. As part of one of those commercialisation projects, I started a spin-out company with three other female academics, and I was the managing director of that company for two years. I completed that phase of my life while also having three children. It was on my third maternity leave that I decided to retrain to be a coach, speaker and trainer, and I've been doing that in my own business since 2019.'

I would then add to this winning introduction the reason I applied for the role.

Technical questions

Technical questions relate to the specific expertise of the role, such as:

- What are the big issues in your area of expertise?

- Describe a time when you created a strategy to achieve a longer-term objective.

- We are keen to develop collaborations between departments. What opportunities for multidisciplinary work do you have?

Opinion questions

Opinion questions often seem to catch people out. They are designed to assess your thoughts and feelings about situations, and ascertain the level of consideration that has gone into applying for the role. For example, 'Describe the culture of your current organisation.' 'Can you give an example of how you work within this culture to achieve a goal?' 'How do you manage stress?' 'What is the first thing you would do in this role?'

Behavioural questions

Behavioural questions are used to test how you view and respond to the world when things don't work. 'Tell me about a time when you changed your priorities to meet others' expectations.' 'Have you been asked to do something that goes against your ethics/ integrity and how did you manage the situation?' 'What has been your greatest disappointment?' 'How did you respond to this?'

Case/situational questions

Case and situational questions are there to find out how resourceful you are, what skills you have, and how you manage situations positively. 'Describe a situation you were involved in that required a multidimensional communication strategy.' 'Tell me about a situation where you had to solve a problem or make a decision that required careful thought. What did you do?' 'Tell me about a time when you improved the way things were typically done on the job.' 'Describe a situation where you needed to influence different stakeholders with differing perspectives.'

It is useful to apply a framework around behavioural, case and situational questions so that you can always formulate one on the spot. A widely cited model for this is the STAR technique, which stands for situation, task, action and result.[17] Describe the situation and when it took place. Explain the task and what the goal was. Provide details about the action you took to achieve this. Conclude with the result of the action. This is a great starting point, but to show a growth mindset I strongly suggest you answer two more questions for additional bonus points. What would you keep the same next time, and what would you do differently?

Brainteaser/abstract questions

The last category is brainteaser and abstract questions. A lot of people I speak to hate these questions, but I must admit I particularly like the abstract ones. They reveal a lot about your personality. 'If you could compare yourself to an animal, which would it be and why?' 'How do you define success?' 'What is one pointless product on the market today?' 'If you had a time machine, would you choose to go to the future or to the past?'

Some of the biggest tech companies on the planet are reported to use brainteaser questions.[18] How do you fare against this Apple brainteaser?[19] 'You have 100 coins lying flat on a table, each with a head side and a tail side. Ten of them are heads-up, ninety are tails-down. You can't feel, see or in any other way find out which ten are heads-up. Your goal: split the coins into two piles so there is the same number of heads-up coins in each pile.' OK, don't run off to find 100 coins just yet, we still have a few more chapters to go, but there's no denying it is a good party trick.

Presenting with presence

We all have a communication style preference which leans towards needing to understand the why, the what, the how, or the what if. When preparing for an interview, whether oral questions or a presentation, make sure all of the why, what, how and what if learners are catered for. For example, in Chapter 7 you heard a client story from Dr Judith Simon. When preparing for her interview with RQM+, she practised a few interview questions with me. I noticed that she bypassed the big-picture why and went straight into an example of what she did. This is because her natural communication preference is for the what. Once she became aware of this bias, she was able to reconstruct her sentences to cover the why learners' perspective first.

Responding to interview questions is not just about putting together practical examples to demonstrate your skills and aptitude. Interviews require mental preparation to get yourself in the best possible state, while minimising fear. Your mind may tell you, 'You need to make a good impression, build a good rapport and answer all the questions correctly.' Often, it feels like so much is at stake, particularly if it is a role that is in ideal alignment with your purpose–mission–vision. Here are my three top preparation tips for presenting yourself with presence so nerves don't get the better of you and ruin the whole experience.

Thoughts on a spot

Start by dealing with the thoughts in your head. There will be a chorus of different selves all offering their concerns and opinions. Look for a mark or spot on the wall, and every time a thought comes up, imagine taking that thought out of your head and putting it on the spot.

'I don't have enough experience.' Put it on the spot on the wall. 'I am so nervous; I won't remember the answer to any of the questions I have prepared.' Put it on the spot on the wall. 'I met one of the people on the interview panel before and they definitely don't like me.' Put it on the spot on the wall. 'If I don't get this job, I'm not going to be able to pay the mortgage.' Put it on the spot on the wall. You get the picture. Keep going until all the voices have been heard, and there are no more opinions to cloud the clarity of your thoughts. You should now have access to clear thinking and brain space.

Expanded awareness

The one thing that fear does is shift us into the past or future, when, to do a great interview, we need to be fully present in the room. I'm sure you've had many experiences of not being fully present: perhaps you've driven somewhere so wrapped up in your thoughts you don't even remember driving the car; maybe you're making food and interacting with the children, but your mind is on solving a work-based problem. We do it all the time, so this is an excellent exercise not just for interview preparation but as a life skill. Why not try dropping into presence right now?

Again, focus on a spot on the wall opposite you, intently for a couple of minutes. Continue to look at the same spot but soften your gaze and expand your awareness to above, below and around the sides of the spot. Keep focusing on the spot but expanding your awareness like a pair of wrap-around glasses. You can even put your hands out to the side and wiggle your fingers to check you can see them, all the while remaining focused on the spot on the wall.

Expanded awareness serves you in several different ways. It brings you right back into the present moment. It is much easier to respond in the moment when you are fully present. It gets you out of the body's hypervigilant, stress, sympathetic nervous system response. When you are in the stress response, your executive functioning is offline, and I'm sure you'll agree being able to use your whole brain is important for an interview.

It is often said that fear and excitement feel the same in the body, but the difference between the two is breath.[20] If you can get your expanded awareness wrap-around glasses on, and breathe with your excited nervousness, then your body will no longer feel under threat. See the excitement as a sign that you are engaged and ready for the interview.

State induction

Once you have those two preparations in place, the final step is to induce the state you want to project. This is not about putting that armour back on, wearing a fake-it-until-you-make-it mask or pretending to be someone you're not. This is about drawing up from inside you the part of you that shines in interviews; the part that talks in an engaging and passionate way;

the part that easily and effortlessly listens and power-fully responds to any questions that arise.

I find music a great access point to state induction. To ebb and flow between engaging and dynamic, calm and commanding, you may want to listen to two pieces of music: one that is upbeat and fills you with inner confidence, such as Demi Lovato's 'Confident', and one that is directive and commanding, perhaps something classical like Tchaikovsky's 'Swan Theme'. Music is subjective though, so do find pieces that work for you.

Below is an excerpt of a transcript from a podcast episode I recorded with Dr Catherine Holden about her experience using these techniques to interview for a new position:

'Yeah, it was our first session and you asked me how did I normally go into interviews, and I told you about how I used to go in with a lot of nervous energy, very positive, very excited, but definitely that anxious nervous energy. And you taught me a few techniques around, I think mostly, it was around learning how to expand my awareness and to embody that different energy going into the interview. One that was calm and confident and just what will be, will be. That was how it felt. So, the thing that I actually did, particularly before the interview, was to go and find a nice peaceful spot in a garden, just close to where I was going to go and meet the panel. I listened to some music. I think it was some Baroque music that you suggested to me. It was not something I necessarily would've picked myself, but it really worked to get me into that frame of mind. So, I listened to that music, and then I did the expanded awareness exercise, and so I went into that interview probably in a completely different way than I ever had done before. Really calm, stately. And yeah, obviously it went really well.'

 Listen to Dr Catherine Holden's full podcast episode here: **https://hannahnikeroberts.com/ inspiring-stories-018-dr-catherine-holden**.

IMPLEMENT THIS

- Develop your winning interview introduction by condensing your qualifications and work experience into two to three clear sentences.

- Map out three case, situational or behavioural interview questions using the expanded STAR technique. Explain the task and what the goal was. Provide details about the action you took to achieve this. Conclude with the result of the action, what you will keep the same next time, and what you will do differently next time.

- Practise the three steps to presenting with presence: thoughts on a spot, expanded awareness and state induction.

10
Propelling Strategies

If you have a pattern of needing to prove yourself in the first twelve months after starting a new job, then it's time for something different. Proving yourself actually works against you, because the internal motivation is fear-driven. Rather than focusing on adding your unique value and talents, actions are wrapped up in little approval-seeking presents: the three not-so-wise gifts of pushing, pleasing and perfecting. Instead, you can accelerate your income, fulfilment and growth by taking ownership of your career transition.

There are four main strategies to focus on when undergoing a career transition: salary negotiation, a 30-60-90-day transition plan, gathering feedback, and creating a personal development plan. Each strategy is of equal importance for ensuring a proactive acceleration as you transition. Think back to your last career transition: were you more proactive or passive in your approach?

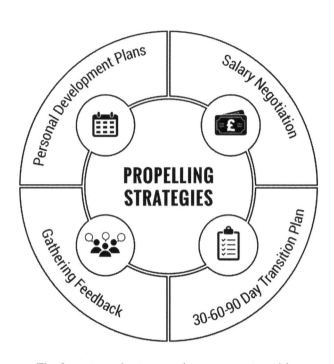

The four strategies to propel your career transition

Closing the gender pay gap

Gender parity is not recovering. According to the *Global Gender Gap Report 2022*, it will take another 132 years to close the global gender pay gap. Although no country has yet achieved full gender parity, the top ten economies have closed at least 80% of their gender gaps, with Iceland leading the global ranking at 90.8%.[1]

Gender equity is a complex issue, consisting of the gender pay gap, the motherhood penalty, the absence of female leaders, working patterns, the leaky pipeline, structural and social barriers, and marginalisation – all of which makes it hard to separate out the gender pay gap from motherhood and other intersectionality issues. If you have made an empowered choice to not have a family or it has not been possible for you, you may feel under-represented in the statistics below, and that is not my intention. I do see and respect you. I have not found a way to separate out specific research on gender from the melee of other related discriminations. You may also wish to look up specific data in your region of the world.

We see headlines in the media making a splash about the gender pay gap being at an all-time low here in the UK. For women aged twenty-two to twenty-nine, in 2022 the gender pay gap stood at 2.1%, and for women aged thirty to thirty-nine, 3.2%. This looks promising, right? Only until you see the gaping gap of 10.9% for women aged forty to forty-nine. It gets worse the older you are: for those over sixty, the gap is 13.9%.[2]

What we are witnessing in these statistics is the result of the increase in the average age women are having children in the UK. More women are having children over the age of thirty-five than under the age of twenty-five. The Office for National Statistics reports that in 1971 just 18% of thirty-year-old women had no children; in 2022 that figure had risen to 50%.[3] This isn't a case of women positively making choices about when to start a family. Childcare in the UK is the second most expensive in the world.[4] For many families, it makes no financial sense for both parents to work, so disproportionately more women end up dropping out of work or reducing their work hours, to care for their children in the five years prior to them starting school. The number of years increases for every additional child in the family. For some women this feels positive; yet for others it's not what they would choose if affordable childcare was available.

CLIENT STORY
Dr Catherine Holden – providing anxiety

We met Dr Catherine Holden in the previous chapter. She is now the automation platform lead at Syngenta and has managed to successfully buck the gender stereotype trend. When she first started working with me at the end of 2019, she was the sole provider for her family as a Marie Skłodowska-Curie postdoctoral fellow. Her husband left his well-paying job to look after their daughter while they relocated to Spain.

As Catherine's position was coming to an end, she felt a lot of pressure to find a job to support her family and provide some stability, but she didn't want to waste all the amazing opportunities and championship she had received from mentors and her husband. She described experiencing anxiety that felt like her tongue was burning. In Catherine's case, it made more sense financially for them as a family to prioritise her career. This anxiety inducing pressure she felt is, unfortunately, the reality of our unaffordable childcare system.

The Fawcett Society states for each year a mother is absent from the workplace her future wages will fall by 4%.[5] Data-driven insights by Resolution Foundation suggest two-thirds of unemployed mothers aren't working because childcare is too expensive, while 67% of mums in work say the cost of childcare prevents them from working more.[6] Many women look for part-time hours or flexibility when they return to work, but are penalised for doing so. It is important to know that, per hour, part-time work is paid less than full-time work, despite the fact that part-time workers can be just as productive and, in my personal experience, more productive, due to the need to complete work within a fixed timescale. Sticking to your designated work hours avoids the resentment trap of working full time (or more) but only being paid a wage for part-time hours. I dread to think what my actual hourly rate was when I worked as a scientific project manager.

Alongside these structure inequities, I find it increasingly frustrating when job adverts fail to post the expected salary range. Only 60% of UK job adverts in 2022 disclosed the position's salary, down from 64% in 2021.[7] The words 'competitive' or 'depending on experience' do not fill me with trust for the organisation. How do you feel when you see these statements? Without a salary range, how can candidates assess whether they want to apply for the role? A Glassdoor study found that 67% of people surveyed felt that salary was one of the top factors that jobseekers look for in ads.[8] This lack of transparency continues to fuel the gender pay gap and inequities in the workforce, whereas an increasing body of evidence shows that

191

if it was law to provide salary details, organisations could attract better and more diverse talent.[9]

When the US banned salary-history questions, pay increased by 5% for job changers overall, 8% for women and 13% for African Americans.[10] As organisational psychologist Adam Grant tweets, 'Pay people what they're worth today, not what they made yesterday.'[11] Until salary transparency becomes law, there is a real need to effectively negotiate both your starting salary and continuous salary increases throughout your career, but how do you actually do that?

Three simple steps to salary negotiation

Leave the salary expectation question blank on application forms and don't mention a specific salary level in your cover letters. You want to get past the screening into the 'to be considered' pile without anyone thinking your anticipated salary is too high.

Ideally, you want your potential employer to make the first offer because it gives a better starting point and more leverage. If you tell them how much you are willing to accept before they make the offer, you are risking overpricing or undervaluing yourself. If you are asked what your salary expectations are before being made a job offer, respond with, 'I will consider any reasonable offer.' If they persist you can reply, 'You are in a much better position to know how much I'm worth to you within your clear organisational structure and salary bands.'

Step one: Preparation

Before you enter any salary negotiations, make sure you have a figure in mind that you want to walk away with: a range including your minimum and the ideal.

Your numbers are not plucked out of thin air; they should be based on thorough research. Recruiters have a fantastic knowledge of current market value. I recommend speaking to at least three recruiters and asking them to name the salary range for a particular role. This is where all your efforts from the professional positioning strategies outlined in Chapter 9 start to pay off, because by now you will have a number of recruiters within your network who you can reach out to.

There are also different websites you can check: Glassdoor,[12] Indeed,[13] LinkedIn,[14] Monster[15] and Check-a-Salary[16] – to name a few. Don't be afraid to reach out to your personal contacts, or ask contacts to act as a broker and introduce you to someone in their network who can advise on a particular role profile. Make sure to enquire about the overall compensation package, not just the salary, as different organisations have additional employee perks which may include: dental treatment, healthcare, amount of annual leave, flexible working, free food and drink, life insurance, wellness packages, training and development, relocation expenses, pension or tax contributions, and home office budget.

Step 2: Negotiation style

When the time comes, request a specific figure. It's been proven that asking for an exact number instead of a range gets you closer to your desired figure.[17] List your worth, including your top career accomplishments, and show ways you have cut costs, increased productivity, saved time, improved a process, made sales, and innovated or enhanced team dynamics. Provide examples using the impact statement formula from Chapter 8. Making this list will also increase your confidence going into the negotiations. Don't forget to negotiate the complete compensation package, including all perks and benefits.[18]

Listen to how the offer is presented, nod your head to signify you are considering it, but keep quiet. The employer could quickly increase the salary in those few moments of silence if they are making lowball offers.

Step 3: Role-play

Step number three is to role-play the salary negotiations with a friend, colleague or coach. It is one of the best ways to prepare and fine-tune your message and your salary overview.

If you are negotiating a pay increase rather than a new starting salary, the same rules apply, but you will be upfront in stating the salary request rather than waiting for an offer. Often, undervalued employees will go for interviews with other organisations and try to use salary offers as leverage in their current organisation. I would urge caution with this technique. Rather than saying, 'If you don't pay me [insert offer] then I will be moving to [insert organisation]', it is more graceful to say, 'I was recently headhunted for an opportunity at [insert organisation]. I'm much more interested in building a career at [insert your current organisation] because I love the mission and values here. Is it possible to have a conversation about my long-term prospects within [insert your current organisation] so that we can put together an effective career development plan?'

Remember, you don't get what you don't ask for and women suffer when they don't negotiate. By not negotiating a first salary, an individual stands to lose more than £500,000 by age sixty, and men are four times as likely as women to negotiate a first salary.[19] The same study calculated that women who consistently negotiate their salary increases earn at least US$1 million more during their careers than women who don't. Who needs the lottery when you have negotiation skills? You are 250 times more likely to be hit by lightning, and eighty times more likely to be attacked by a shark than win the lottery.[20] Negotiation is not just a technique for transitioning, but an ongoing strategy for an intentional career.[21]

30-60-90-day transition plans

Dr Isaiah Hankel, founder of Cheeky Scientist, coined the term '30-60-90-day transition plan' as a way of taking ownership of career transition rather than turning up at a new place of work and waiting to be taught and developed.[22]

During the first thirty days, learn how things operate, and focus on understanding the tools and systems of the organisation by asking yourself these questions:

- Where do I find things?

- How can I access them?

- How can I use them to get the job done?

- Who can help me?

Learn the culture of the organisation and gain knowledge of the product or the service. Build rapport with people and take on a small project.

In the first sixty days, plan to start working with your team(s) and you will be seen as an asset. You can do this by taking on a big project and gaining mentorship from your manager and other employees. Make sure you understand the unwritten rules and structure of the organisation. There will be an organisational chart and policies and procedures but how are things *really* done? What practices are actually in use?

By the end of your first ninety days, fully integrate yourself, be of value, and succeed in your role by juggling bigger responsibilities and taking on an independent big project with minimal supervision. Connect and build relationships with key people in your team, as well as with departmental peers and cross-functional members. Don't forget to forge relationships with people at all levels, especially those who can mentor and sponsor you.

Transition plans also work for internal promotions. Dr Lucy Woods first started working with me at the beginning of 2022 as business unit manager for metabolomics at Bruker Daltonics. By the end of 2022, she had signed her new contract with Bruker as a commercial director and secured an exciting move from the UK to Singapore.

Even though Lucy knew the company and products well, having worked at Bruker for over seven years, following the 30-60-90-day transition plan clarified where to focus her attention. She was already aware of the first 30-day, small-scale project, and following the plan gave her the confidence to pursue this as a priority.

 Listen to Lucy's full podcast episode at **www. hannahnikeroberts.com/inspiring-stories-032-dr-lucy-woods**.

Growing through feedback

According to the book *Change or Die: The three keys to change at work and in life*, we are hardwired to do one of two things: move towards pleasure or away from pain.[23] When it comes to our mistakes and shortcomings, our default is to do anything to avoid the pain of addressing failure. As a result, we often blame others, make excuses or suppress the vulnerability the failure has caused. Using emotional intelligence involves enquiry into your psychology, thoughts, emotions, reactions and behaviours.

In 2005, I graduated with a first-class MChem from The University of Manchester and was accepted onto Croda's graduate development scheme. During the first year, I attended a five-day personal development residential. Featured alongside swinging from the trees were professional skills and tasks, such as presenting your work, and team communication dynamics. After my presentation, I received a piece of candid feedback from another participant: 'Your presentation style reminds me of cabin crew giving the safety briefing on a flight.' Even with lashings of positive intent, that piece of feedback felt like an unjustified gut punch. Mistakes stay as mistakes if we don't have the opportunity to learn from them. That's why being taught how to give and receive effective feedback is critical in this process.

During a career transition, it is essential to gather feedback from your colleagues to inform your next yearly personal and professional development plan. One of the most precious gifts we can receive is feedback given within a constructive framework. If you feel ready to engage in the concept of data-driven human performance, popularised by 360-degree feedback loops, create a type form with the following questions, and push it out via direct email and social media to friends, family and co-workers:[24]

- Your name

- The nature of our relationship (how do you know me?)

- How long have you known me?

- Describe my strengths

- Describe my blind spots

- What do you understand are my goals?

- What is your prediction of my success or failure in achieving those goals?

- What advice would you like to give me?

Increasing the amount of feedback we ask for and receive can be scary, but it means more data points to learn and grow from, which ultimately increases our motivation and places us firmly back in a position of powerful action. When Dr Verena Wolfram was transitioning from her role as technical advisor at NICE to senior medical affairs manager of scientific engagement at Pfizer, she found this exercise enlightening. As a result of the feedback she received, in the first six months of her new role she focused on applying a framework to gather other people's perspectives when making strategic decisions.

Yet another qualification?

Take the time to review your natural talents and skills and work on your personal development plan. The idea is to master your natural talents, because a key component of feeling fulfilled is excellence in the work you are doing. You may also need to become competent in other skills to be effective in your role. For example, you may take Lean Six Sigma Training to learn the art of successive process improvement, thereby mastering your talent for challenging the status quo. If you work in an organisation that uses Agile project management but you are not a project manager yourself, you may read a book on Agile to gain insights into the lexicon and the system, rather than taking the full certification process.

CLIENT STORY
Dr Zohra Butt – to MBA or not to MBA, that's the question

Over the course of twelve months of coaching, Dr Zohra Butt identified that her natural talents and vision aligned to the profession of medical scientific liaison. I witnessed her time and time again on LinkedIn, building a new professional community and reaching out to contacts for informal interviews. It was fantastic to see her commitment to creating a new opportunity.

She was offered maternity leave cover in the role of medical science liaison at Pierre Fabre UK. Within three months, a permanent position was created for her. In her last one-to-one coaching session with me, she expressed a desire to do a master's in business administration (MBA) and wanted to understand whether it was something she wanted or another example of needing a certificate or qualification to be taken seriously.

Zohra relayed an example from the past where she had to use the statement, 'During my eight years' experience working in oncology I found that . . .' just to get the other person to properly listen to her. She knew she had something of value to say, but the implicit biases against her being a woman, and a woman of colour, were all too common. Her parents even used to say, 'No one can take your qualifications away from you.'

I asked her to talk through her long-term vision, and we discovered those at director level had a clinical, pharmaceutical or business qualification. An MBA was aligned with her vision and would make that pathway smoother and easier. Next, we reviewed her Talent Dynamics profile to see if the MBA would give her mastery of her natural talents or whether competency level would suffice; for example by reading a book series or taking a mini online course. The MBA would enhance one of her secondary strength profiles to mastery level and allow her to become competent in a skill set and lexicon she had the motivation to learn.

Another concern was that she was always looking for the next thing and couldn't just be happy with what is. Right there in her top five values was growth, so it made sense that she was always seeking new growth opportunities, motivated by a positive towards-motivation rather than getting-away-from feelings of inadequacy.

Knowing her vision, natural talents and values, Zohra gained the clarity she needed. An MBA was right for her, and she went ahead with asking for financial support and time from her company. That was an empowered decision, not one run on heady fumes of fear. Do take the time to assess your motivations if another qualification looks enticing. How much of the desire is alignment, and how much of it is fear-driven?

Far too often, I have seen people taking master's after master's to gain knowledge of different sectors, to feel comfortable applying for positions. There comes a point in your education where you can learn any topic you are interested in without the need for a formal qualification (unless it is necessary for professional regulation). Take action to find out if that qualification will elevate you to where you want to be or enhance your natural talents before committing thousands of pounds, just in case.

IMPLEMENT THIS

- Before a job interview, do your research on starting salaries and the range you are willing to accept for the role. Use Glassdoor (or other websites) and recruiters, and don't be afraid to ask people who do that role what salary range to expect.

- Create your feedback type form and push it out to at least ten people in positions in a variety of levels. Use the results to inform your next personal development plan. Mine the feedback for gold and look at what implementation support you might need.

- Review your personality profile and look for ways to master your natural talents and become competent at other skills, driven by the context of the organisation.

- Create your 30-60-90-day transition plan.

11
Making It Happen

Our emotions, beliefs, habits and behaviours have got us this far, but they are now holding us back from being the true and authentic expression of ourselves. We need to overcome the obstacles that get in the way of having an intentional career. It's not enough to know the path; we must walk it. That journey is much easier when you have someone walking by your side.

What I have shared with you may seem simple because I've given you just six things to focus on, but never underestimate the power of simplicity.

You'll start to see these ideas everywhere, now you know them. I can guarantee that over the next twelve months my inbox will be full of people emailing me their success stories as a result of following the Career Pivots Compass. I already know what they will say: 'I prioritised myself and my own career trajectory and took micro-actions each and every week, and now I have created balance, confidence and fulfilment. I'm actually happy!'

I sincerely want *you* to be in that group. I want your story in my inbox telling me you've done these six simple things and made yourself an opportunity magnet; that your health and relationships have improved and your confidence increased; that you're feeling fulfilled and at peace with yourself.

Will you succeed?

Sadly, there's a good chance you won't be feeling content. Worry, resentment and comparisonitis are three major energy thieves. The worrying thing about worry is that most of us would rather worry than act on something. Indecision leads to worry. We say, 'I just need to think about it for a while.' None of that is thinking, it is worrying dressed up as thinking, in high heels and a leopard print coat. Then we say, 'Let me think about that some more.' Being intentional in our lives requires action and decisions. In Dr Joanna Martin's words, 'Our success in life is in direct proportion to the velocity with which we make decisions.'[1]

Maybe you are even a little bit addicted to the anxiety of worry, to the struggle. Why make things easy when you can complicate things? I was driving back from a workshop (I seem to spend a lot of time on the M5/M6 corridor) and I needed the toilet, but I wasn't desperate. I spotted the 'services in one mile' sign. Did I do the sensible thing? No. I whizzed straight past the turn-off and had to wait another 36 miles, by which time I was busting for a wee. I've had three children and one side of my pelvic floor muscles was severely damaged after a ventouse delivery with Oscar. By the time I reached the service toilets, I had wet knickers and had to take them off. Luckily, I know the people reading this book are not the type to troll me on social media for this revelation. There was no rationale for not taking that first exit, but the will-I-won't-I-make-it worry is perversely exciting. Do you know the type of worry I'm talking about? Procrastination until the deadline is so close the fear has become valid.

Do you let complexity get in the way of simplicity, the nonurgent, important stuff for other people usurping your highest priorities? With this approach you will remain stuck or, worse, the desire for quick and easy wins will creep in and you'll take the next opportunity presented to you, hoping a fresh start will be the answer. It rarely is. Much better to take the time to define what you want and align yourself fully to that. You don't need it all mapped out perfectly using colour-coded pens. As lovely as that sounds, all you need to do is take the first step in the right direction using the Career Pivots Compass.

I've been studying human behaviour my whole life and have developed a deep understanding of it as a coach. I will share with you some of the things I've noticed when watching people make successful career pivots as opposed to those who are perpetually paralysed and frozen in the headlights of life. I'll share ideas on how to overcome these obstacles so you can value yourself, be valued by others and make a valuable contribution to the world, with ease.

You'll do it faster with support

When left alone, most people become distracted, bored, disheartened and unmotivated; they will not complete any of the Career Pivots Compass methodology to fulfil their true potential. If you are saying to yourself, 'When I finish this project, then I will focus on my career,' unfortunately it will never happen because one thing quickly becomes replaced by another and time marches on despite you feeling undervalued, overworked and underpaid. It's like waiting for the perfect wave before you get in the water to start surfing.

Not only are the conditions never perfect for action, but most people become so used to being in career inertia that when it comes to the time to act, they don't do anything.

I've met hundreds of postdocs who continue to another three-year contract, hoping that something will be different this time. They vehemently cling to the hope that luck will be on their side and everything will fall into place on that academic conveyor belt. I like to ask individuals who are feeling stuck in their careers, 'How long are you willing to give to this role? What is your absolute cut-off point?' I remember a postdoc once telling me she was two years in to her first three-year postdoc, and that if after three fellowship applications she had not been awarded a fellowship, or the last twelve months of the postdoc expired, she would activate a new pathway beyond academia. Do you need to give yourself a firm cut-off point? If yes, what will the criteria be?

The truth is, it's harder to reach your full potential on your own. That's why, when I swam for England juniors and did the Olympic trials, I had a coach. That's why presidents and prime ministers have advisors, and musicians have conductors to bring out their best performances.

As an approximate range, it is recommended that you allocate 3–5% of your annual income for training and development.[2] This will depend of course on the access to training you have at your current place of work, how many years of personal and professional development you have already missed, and your own personal set of circumstances surrounding money. Regardless, I have found development and growth always pay dividends. Billionaire investor Warren Buffet says, 'Ultimately, there's one investment that supersedes all others: invest in yourself. It's an investment no one can take away from you, it can't be taxed and not even inflation can take it away from you.'[3]

Having support inspires you into action and once you are in motion it is easier to stay in momentum. Simple laws of physics. When you meet resistance from your limiting beliefs, emotions and old patterns of behaviours, that's when coaching comes into its own and quickly helps you get unstuck and moving forwards again. A coach believes in you until you are capable of fully believing in yourself. They can see where you are not playing all out and create the space for awareness and change.

CLIENT STORY
Anna Fuller – the inside-out revolution

Anna Fuller is a prime example of this. She made the big bold decision to quit her job as a research laboratory manager with three months' notice period because, as she put it, 'On 1 January 2023 I will be in a new one.' After a flurry of activity applying for roles, a failed interview left her feeling dejected and concerned. As a result, she hadn't applied for a single job in two weeks, despite seeing job alerts which were aligned with her purpose–mission–vision. She was three-out-of-ten confident that on Wednesday evening she would apply for another role. Cleaning the house was looking more appealing. (I can relate to this, having painted my house to avoid writing my PhD thesis.) What is your go-to procrastination task?

On the next Career Design Mastermind group coaching call, she brought this challenge for laser coaching. You might be surprised to hear that I didn't go straight in with setting targets and more accountability, because that doesn't work when we are emotionally blocked.

At first, Anna's internal dialogue was an Inner Critic telling-off: 'You have to do this, you didn't do it last time you said you would. Get on with it.' Then the internal dialogue shifted into something else – the worry she would get to January without a job, and all the Protector Controller 'what-ifs' circling around her brain: 'It's going to look bad. I've made this bold move, bold statement, and what if I don't pull it off? Everyone who knows me knows I've done this so everyone will know. I'll look ignorant for doing that and not seeing it through. Then I worry about going for interviews and them saying, "When are you available?", and I have to say, "I'm available now," because I don't have a job. I don't think that sounds good and I feel like I'm not going to be so confident going into an interview in that weak position. That's a really big deal.'

I asked the question, 'Who are you most concerned about knowing?' Anna replied, 'I wouldn't want my current colleagues to find out I haven't got another job. I discovered I have been thinking that I'm better than this, so if I don't go and get another job, I'm not better than that and I probably should have stayed. They will all know that I'm not better than that.'

I enquired about the feeling inside that comes with the thought, 'What if I'm not better than this?' Anna said, 'It's kind of upsetting because this is somewhere I'm not happy, and I don't want to think that this is what I'm stuck with, because that's what it would feel like.'

I summarised, 'If we know you are going to feel really upset, icky and trapped inside if you don't pull this off in the timeframe you are looking for, what is it that you need to believe about yourself to get back into application action?' Anna paused for a moment then answered, 'An authentic belief that I'm good enough rather than this egotistical belief that I'm better than this. This belief gives me confidence in myself and what I can do.'

Once we change our internal narrative, we can more easily make changes in our external lives. I checked this was the case for Anna: 'If you came from the position of this true authentic self that has the belief of "I am good enough", would you be able to take action to move beyond this current situation?' Anna said, 'Yes, I would. I remember being really confident a few months ago when making applications and that confidence shined through then.'

I reminded her that this internal belief was actually what led her to make the big bold statement to quit her job in the first place, and did a final check to see if she needed anything to integrate that belief and get back into action. Sometimes clients may need tools or techniques to support actions. Anna said she was 8 out of 10 confident she would apply for a job on Wednesday and asked for an accountability check-in. She initiated a check-in three days later to tell us she did indeed get back into action and applied for another aligned job.

I know you can do this alone, but with the right kind of support you will do this at speed and be able to tap into resources within yourself you didn't know existed. This means results that were not conceivable to you before. That is the journey of the intentional career unhindered by personal limitations.

Be the change you want to see in the world

It was the summer of 2011, and I paced the fourth-floor chemistry corridor at The University of Manchester, stopping periodically to study group photos so faded they appeared brown and white. It hit me like a bolt of lightning. Row upon row of men.

I looked intently to see if I could find someone like me, anyone who looked like me. As I scanned the next photo and the next, I became acutely aware once again of the little bean growing inside me. 'Just stay calm,' I told myself. 'Breathe and slow down your heart rate, you will be fine when you get in there.'

Three months earlier I'd had a miscarriage and this new seven-week-old miracle was a secret. Finally, at the end of the corridor, having scanned the whole row, I stopped. This photo of chemistry graduates was the only one that had some women at the front, and I wondered if any of them had done a PhD viva when pregnant.

It was time. I'd heard stories of people being in and out in anything from ninety minutes to seven hours with major corrections. I quickly realised it wasn't about the experiments; I had ten published publications. It was a thought experiment, testing how you think your way through to a solution. As is customary, I left the room to await the verdict. Back in the corridor, it felt like those women in the photo were smiling at me.

There is still much trailblazing to be done when it comes to DEI and justice. I feel like the tide is turning though, and I have seen this shift in my own lifetime, although not at the pace I would like. Malala Yousafzai overcame an assassination attempt by the Taliban in occupied Pakistan at the age of fifteen, and went on to campaign for women's rights and children's rights to an education.[4] Michelle Obama was the first African American First Lady of the US.[5] Jacinda Arden was in office as prime minister of New Zealand from 2017 to 2023, during which time she saw her country through a global pandemic, the Christchurch Mosque attacks, the Whakaari/White Island volcano eruption, domestic and political malaise, and gave birth to her daughter.[6] Greta Thunberg is the Swedish environmental activist who has challenged world leaders to take immediate action for climate change mitigation.[7]

We look ahead to these trailblazers as role models, but please do not forget that the next generation coming through are looking at you, at the way you operate, your work pattern, how you conduct yourself in meetings, from big to small things and everything in between. What you do and how you behave matters.

Leadership is not about turning individuals into heroes though. True leaders are able to lead, follow and walk alongside others; to be in collaboration rather than competition; to speak up with integrity and to ask for the support needed. We must all be leaders of ourselves first. In doing so, you may just inadvertently become a leader in a different capacity too.

CLIENT STORY
Dr Georgina Washington – putting your head above the parapet

When I first started working with Georgina, she had been identified as a rising talent in her organisation. She was invited to participate in and lead a session in an event designed to promote recruitment opportunities and attract new talent to the organisation.

Georgina loves showcasing to others that you can be a woman in a senior technical role, and you can make it work while having a young family too. It's something she is passionate about, so she agreed to support the initiative.

The evening before the event, an email confirmed the childcare setting Georgina used was going to be closed the next day due to an extreme weather event. After consultation, the organising committee agreed Georgina could bring her child to the event, and she dutifully spent the rest of the evening putting together a bag of toys to keep them occupied for the day.

As she arrived on site with her child the next day, Georgina was greeted by a staff member who said to have her child there would be inappropriate. Having moved what felt like heaven and earth to be there, Georgina felt discarded and unable to contain her emotions. She spent the majority of the day crying in her office. She worried her emotions had betrayed her and others would not see her as mature enough to be in her role, that they would question her capability and, ultimately, that she would no longer be thought of as someone with further leadership potential.

During our coaching session, Georgina wanted to understand how to get over her emotions more quickly and express herself clearly to others. We discovered, through coaching questions, it wasn't about the time and effort spent on logistics and not being able to participate – that was neither here nor there. It turned out that in the moment of being relieved of her duties, her strong value for integrity was rocked to its core.

One of the reasons she had joined the company was its stance on DEI. She had always found the company to be flexible and supportive of her career aspirations. This was an example of a moment when, through her eyes, the company was not demonstrating integrity. DEI and flexible working promises were used as incentives to recruit people, but then not lived out in the moment during the recruitment event.

Now that we had explored the reasons why she had such an emotional reaction, I asked Georgina if she felt her reaction was too big. The answer was no. Georgina decided that to continue to work within the organisation, she needed to have an honest conversation with her senior leadership team, to tell them that DEI needed to be factored in at the earliest stage, not as an afterthought. For example, the event itself started at 8.30am and some parts were in the evening and at the weekend, which made it difficult for working parents to attend without putting children in additional childcare. By adding the weight of her voice, she could clear the pathway for a new approach.

I had to be honest: one of two different things could happen as a result of speaking out. The organisation might fully engage with Georgina's ideas and move forwards or, if the company was not open to change, then they might do nothing. Georgina said if the latter happened she would no longer want to work for them out of integrity and would move to another organisation.

Courage isn't something you need to build up to enable you to take courageous action. Courage is something you create as a direct result of doing the thing you are fearful of. What actually happened when Georgina spoke out was an agreement that the department values had not been lived up to in that moment.

The company concluded it was a good time to adjust the way the event was organised according to the values and commitments of the organisation, as a new person had just been appointed to lead the event. An agreement to have an ongoing review to make change easier to achieve in the long-term was forged. Georgina now feels positive about the future because she is back honouring her personal integrity and will continue to speak out.

Your emotions always point to the truth if you are willing to feel and explore them. They may just set you on a new and more aligned course of action.

IMPLEMENT THIS

- Worry, resentment and comparisonitis are three major energy thieves. Are these energy thieves active in your life? What percentage of your time and energy do they rob you of?
- How long are you willing to stay in your current role?
- What criteria constitute your absolute cut-off point?'
- What would you like to achieve in your life financially in the next twelve months?
- What access to personal and professional development do you have currently at your place of work?

- Do you have the support you need to take your next career pivot or will you need to look at external provisions? For example, do you have a mentor, coach or sponsor, and access to resource development?

- If you need an external provision, review your income and expenditure. What percentage of your income can you allocate to personal and professional development in the next twelve months? Most banks will allow you to set up an automatic separate savings space.

Conclusion

Congratulations on reading this book, taking steps towards figuring out 'what's next?' in your career and finding the strategy to make it happen. I'm sure you have started to appreciate and value yourself more as a result. Your career is there to enhance your experience of life, not diminish it.

This book has clear themes within it. You have read about time and energy management, overcoming your personal limitations, following your natural talents to create a leadership pathway, connecting the dots of your purpose–mission–vision, creating opportunities using professional positioning, and propelling strategies – all of which will enable you to be proactive in your Intentional Careers journey.

You have read my story and been inspired by my clients. Now it's your turn. Maya Angelou writes,

'There is no greater agony than bearing an untold story inside you.'[1] It's time. Write the next chapter of your life unhindered by past experiences and failures. Own your story and you will no longer be defined by it.

I see a world where every member of society is valued equally for their contribution and everyone is respected. You count. You are valued. You matter more than you will ever know.

If you want to feel loved, you must first learn how to love yourself.

If you want to improve your relationship with others, you must first learn how to improve your relationship with yourself.

If you want to be respected by others, you must first learn how to respect yourself.

What is the lesson you need to learn that will set you free from the cage you are trapped in?

Next Steps

It was 7 March 2014 and I was six hours into labour. Just an hour ago, gas and air had been the most amazing invention ever; now it barely touched the sides. I gripped the plastic tube with my teeth, the bite indentations a clear sign I was rapidly losing my mental reserve.

The transition phase. Little did I know I was only three contractions away from pushing Jenson out. I had hit the pain wall. How on earth could I keep going? I remember going somewhere deep in the depths of my mind, resetting and concentrating on a spot on the wall. A new inner resolve.

There will be times before the end of this year when you hit the metaphorical wall. Remember, it's not your final destination. Keep showing up, moving through and opening up to more. Future you will thank you for it.

If you would like support with your Intentional Careers journey, there are three resources I recommend.

1. **Intentional Careers Scorecard:** What you measure gets improved, and this set of questions is designed to score you on the six areas of the Career Pivots Compass. It gives you data-driven insights in a personalised report and access to further training videos so you can speed up your progress. Visit **https://scorecard.intentional-careers.com/ strategy**.

2. **Intentional Careers workshop:** A powerful ninety-minute workshop on the six strategies to figuring out 'what's next?' in your career and the strategy to make it happen, while balancing the things and people that mean most to you. Register for your free place here: **www.intentional-careers.com/ workshop**.

3. **Career Design Mastermind:** Our flagship six-month programme is designed for STEM and professional women to design a career for fulfilment with a mindset for leadership. Visit **www.intentional-careers.com/cdmm**.

Intentional Career
Case Study Journeys

Dr Catherine Holden

When I first met Dr Catherine Holden, she was finishing up her Marie Skłodowska-Curie Individual Fellowship in Spain. Her husband had left his well-paying job to look after their daughter while living in Spain which designated Catherine the sole provider for their family. She was feeling a lot of anxiety and pressure to find a job that could support their family and provide stability without wanting to waste all of the amazing opportunities and support she had received from her husband and mentors.

Early in our coaching journey, she had two successful interviews: one for an Independent Fellowship in academia and another for a Team Leader role at Syngenta. By mapping out the blueprint for what would make her happy and fulfilled in her career she made the choice to listen to her instincts and go for the Team Leader position at Syngenta. Within eighteen months, while on maternity leave, she was promoted to Platform Lead in Automation Chemistry.

 Listen to Dr Catherine Holden sharing her coaching journey at: **https://hannahnikeroberts.com/ inspiring-stories-018-dr-catherine-holden**.

Dr Natsuko Suwaki

Dr Natsuko Suwaki joined a series of nine lunch and learn workshops I facilitated for GSK's Women's Leadership Initiative during the early months of the pandemic. When Natsuko first contacted me, she was the Global Labelling Delivery Manager at GSK and always felt that other people had incredible opportunities land on their laps whereas she was feeling stuck and simultaneously wanting more.

By focusing on her natural talents and strengths, she made a sideways move to operations manager in the ethics and compliance function before being promoted within twelve months to Governance and Standards Director in Legal and Compliance. In addition, she has found the capacity to take on a big vision passion project in the DEI space and doing all of this while improving relationships and balance at home too.

Listen to Dr Natsuko Suwaki sharing her coaching journey at: **https://hannahnikeroberts.com/ inspiring-stories-016-natsuko-suwaki**.

Dr Verena Wolfram

I met Dr Verena Wolfram exactly one year after she adopted her two children. She was working as an assessment analyst for NICE on a 0.8 full-time equivalent contract. Although she had created a good work–life balance, something didn't feel quite right, and she kept searching for the next career opportunity without really knowing what she wanted.

During our coaching sessions, Verena processed the grief of not being able to have biological children and the grief of fully letting go of her academic identity, allowing her to take the next steps in her career. Understanding her values and natural talents resulted in her initiating a twelve-month internal secondment as a technical advisor in the Office for Digital Health at NICE, before successfully pivoting to senior medical affairs manager in scientific engagement at Pfizer.

 Listen to Dr Verena Wolfram sharing her coaching journey at: **https://hannahnikeroberts.com/ inspiring-stories-021-verena-wolfram**.

Dr Rachel Dunmore

Dr Rachel Dunmore fell into project management in HR after a postdoc and period of burnout at The University of York. Rachel initially wanted to master the foundational layer of time and energy management to defend against burnout relapse.

Rachel became what I refer to as a productivity ninja, learning how to prioritise important tasks and protect focus time. Once she felt more resourced, she was able to tackle her lack of passion for work. She discovered that her natural talents aligned with the role profile, but through connecting the dots of her purpose–mission–vision it became clear her vision was disconnected from her workplace. Using her vision as a navigational tool, she identifies organisations that are a match and takes action to create the opportunities she is looking for long-term.

 Listen to Dr Rachel Dunmore sharing her coaching journey at: **https://hannahnikeroberts.com/ inspiring-stories-017-dr-rachel-dunmore**.

Dr Natasha Rhys

When I first started working with Dr Natasha Rhys she was employed as a King's Prize Research Fellow at King's College London. A series of life events had rocked her confidence and she wanted to focus on improving her career and confidence.

What made the most profound difference was uncovering the underlying limiting beliefs and patterns of behaviour which were replaying out in multiple different areas of her life. By implementing tools and techniques to deal with the underlying emotional allergies, she identified her true purpose and took her first career pivot as an independent researcher development consultant. Having gathered insights from this experience, she is now working on integrating her natural talents into her next career pivot.

 Listen to Dr Natasha Rhys sharing her coaching journey at: **https://hannahnikeroberts.com/ inspiring-stories-025-dr-natasha-rhys**.

Dr Ciara Keating

Dr Ciara Keating was a member of the Vis-NET project funded by the Engineering and Physical Sciences Research Council, designed to reinvent the rules of international collaborations and reduce gender differences in academic careers. I was delivering a series of personal and professional skills training sessions to the consortium and Ciara approached me about coaching to improve her situation. As a postdoc at Glasgow University, she was working a seventy-hour week, which was affecting her health, and she was not being considered for an internal lectureship despite meeting all of the essential criteria.

During our coaching sessions, she learned how to set boundaries with her time and with other people to manage the diagnosis of endometriosis and fibromyalgia. She had plenty of practice at implementing nonconfrontational conversation templates, such as saying no, asking for needs, boundary setting, and learning how to effectively speak up.

 Listen to Dr Ciara Keating sharing her coaching journey at: **https://hannahnikeroberts.com/ inspiring-stories-024-dr-ciara-keating**.

Dr Kaneenika Sinha

Dr Kaneenika Sinha is an associate professor of mathematics at the Indian Institute of Science Education and Research in Pune. Kaneenika joined a workshop I conducted on energy and effectiveness for the Women in Science network at Banaras Hindu University and subsequently began her coaching journey. She was vacillating between two contradictory feelings: the excitement presented by future research possibilities versus despondency and overwhelm that came with questions such as, 'Is this it? Will I go further?'

Thanks to Kaneenika's period of coaching and self-reflection, this chapter of her life has turned into the most important and fulfilling phase of her academic journey. She learned how to focus on a few chosen research projects related to her vision, setting healthy boundaries and learning how to say no as well as dealing with the constant stream of critical feedback that comes with the territory of academia. Most importantly, she has learned how to seek internal validation rather than letting the Inner Critic control the narrative in her brain.

 Listen to Dr Kaneenika Sinha sharing her coaching journey at: **https://hannahnikeroberts. com/inspiring-stories-019-dr-kaneenika-sinha- client-story**.

Dr Judith Simon

The COVID-19 pandemic has often been called the big pause. A time when people were able to slow down long enough to see what was and wasn't working in their lives. As a postdoc, Dr Judith Simon had the revelation that it was time to move beyond academia and embarked on coaching to support that transition and stop the slip back into bad working habits.

Judith had to process an emotional journey before being able to interview for new positions so that she didn't have 'one foot in and one foot out' syndrome. She defined her career values and used them as a template for fulfilment in the transition from postdoc to medical writer. In addition, understanding her natural talents motivated her to seize the opportunity to apply for an internal promotion within the first six months of working as a Senior Consultant at RQM+.

Listen to Dr Judith Simon sharing her coaching journey at: **https://hannahnikeroberts.com/ inspiring-stories-022-dr-judith-simon**.

Additional client stories can be found at **https:// hannahnikeroberts.com/podcast**, and you can tune in on your favourite podcast platform.

Notes

Introduction

1 The Intentional Careers model and its affiliated products are trademarks.
2 The Career Pivots and affiliated products are registered trademarks.

Chapter 1: Careers Fit For The Third Millennium

1 Z Khan (@zaidleppelin), 'Quiet quitting'
(25 July 2022), www.tiktok.com/@zaidleppelin/
video/7124414185282391342, accessed 24 December 2022
2 L Goler, J Gale, B Harrington and A Grant, 'The 3 things
employees really want: Career, community, cause',
Harvard Business Review (20 February 2018), https://hbr.
org/2018/02/people-want-3-things-from-work-but-most-
companies-are-built-around-only-one, accessed 25 May
2023

3 World Health Organization, 'Coronavirus disease (COVID-19) pandemic' (no date), www.who.int/europe/emergencies/situations/covid-19, accessed 22 December 2022

4 A Stuart, 'Goats take over empty Welsh streets during coronavirus lockdown', *The Guardian* (31 March 2020), www.theguardian.com/uk-news/video/2020/mar/31/goats-take-over-empty-welsh-streets-llandudno-coronavirus-lockdown-video, accessed 22 December 2022

5 D Carrington, 'Coronavirus UK lockdown causes big drop in air pollution', *The Guardian* (27 March 2020), www.theguardian.com/environment/2020/mar/27/coronavirus-uk-lockdown-big-drop-air-pollution, accessed 22 December 2022

6 Gallup, *State of the Global Workplace: 2022 report*, www.gallup.com/workplace/349484/state-of-the-global-workplace.aspx, accessed 14 February 2023

7 P Kane, 'The Great Resignation is here, and it's real', *Inc.* (26 August 2021), www.inc.com/phillip-kane/the-great-resignation-is-here-its-real.html, accessed 21 November 2022

8 L Weber, 'Forget going back to the office – people are just quitting instead', *The Wall Street Journal* (13 June 2021), www.wsj.com/articles/forget-going-back-to-the-officepeople-are-just-quitting-instead-11623576602, accessed 21 November 2022

9 J Haden, 'The Great Resignation: Why millions of people are quitting (and how employers can earn them back)', *Inc.* (10 August 2021), www.inc.com/jeff-haden/great-resignation-employees-quitting-attract-great-employees-wage-rates-signing-bonuses.html, accessed 21 November 2022

10 J Fuller and W Kerr, 'The Great Resignation didn't start with the pandemic', *Harvard Business Review* (23 March 2022), https://hbr.org/2022/03/the-great-resignation-didnt-start-with-the-pandemic, accessed 22 November 2022

11 J Boys, 'The Great Resignation – fact or fiction?', *CIPD Voice* (21 February 2022), www.cipd.org/uk/views-and-insights/thought-leadership/cipd-voice/great-resignation-fact-fiction, accessed 22 November 2022

12 Accenture UK, 'COVID-19 set women's gains back
    by decades' (8 March 2021), www.accenture.com/
    gb-en/blogs/blogs-women-gains-back, accessed
    22 November 2022

13 M Armstrong, 'It will take another 136 years to close the
    global gender gap' (World Economic Forum, 12 April 2021),
    www.weforum.org/agenda/2021/04/136-years-is-the-
    estimated-journey-time-to-gender-equality, accessed
    23 November 2022

14 Pregnant Then Screwed, *The Impact of Covid-19*
    (8 June 2020), www.docdroid.net/joYdZsN/the-impact-of-
    covid-19docx-pdf, accessed 6 February 2022

15 University of Liverpool, 'Prosper: Unlocking postdoc career
    potential' (no date), www.liverpool.ac.uk/researcher/
    prosper, accessed 12 May 2022

16 P Grange, *Fear Less: How to win at life without losing yourself*
    (Vermilion, 2020)

17 R Fry, 'Millennials are the largest generation in the
    US labor force' (Pew Research Center, 11 April 2018),
    www.pewresearch.org/short-reads/2018/04/11/
    millennials-largest-generation-us-labor-force, accessed
    16 February 2023

18 A Lettink, 'No, millennials will not be 75% of the
    workforce in 2025 (or ever)!' (LinkedIn Newsletter,
    17 September 2019), www.linkedin.com/pulse/
    millennials-75-workforce-2025-ever-anita-lettink, accessed
    7 March 2022

19 Ibid

20 A Adkins, 'Millennials: The job-hopping generation'
    (Gallup Workplace, no date), www.gallup.com/
    workplace/231587/millennials-job-hopping-generation,
    accessed 7 March 2022

21 D Farrell, 'Exit, voice, loyalty and neglect as responses
    to job dissatisfaction: A multidimensional scaling study',
    Academy of Management Journal, 26/4 (December 1983), 596–
    607, www.jstor.org/stable/255909, accessed 5 April 2023

22 The VOICE model and its affiliated products/solutions/
    platforms are trademarks.

23 B1G1 Business for Good: https://b1g1.com, accessed
    17 April 2023

24 500 Women Scientists, 'Fellowship for the Future:
    Recognizing women of color leading in STEM' (no date),

https://500womenscientists.org/fellowship-for-the-future-about, accessed 17 April 2023

25 S Harrison and L Sweetingham, *Thirst: A story of redemption, compassion, and a mission to bring clean water to the world* (Currency, 2018)

26 A Adamczyk, 'Millennials own less than 5% of all US wealth' (CNBC, 9 October 2020), www.cnbc.com/2020/10/09/millennials-own-less-than-5percent-of-all-us-wealth, accessed 16 February 2023; R Wearmouth, 'Baby boomers hoarding half of Britain's wealth while young are worse off, says think tank' (HuffPost, 20 June 2017), www.huffingtonpost.co.uk/entry/resolution-found-boomers_uk_5947f1fae4b0cddbb0085500, accessed 16 February 2023

27 R Fry, 'The pace of Boomer retirements has accelerated in the past year' (Pew Research Center, 9 November 2020), www.pewresearch.org/fact-tank/2020/11/09/the-pace-of-boomer-retirements-has-accelerated-in-the-past-year, accessed 30 October 2022

28 H Roberts, 'Think back to process' (LinkedIn survey, October 2022), www.linkedin.com/feed/update/urn:li:activity:6980091338985721856, accessed 5 January 2023

Chapter 2: Taking Ownership Of Your Career

1 *How My Body Works*, series (Orbis, 1994)
2 The Career Design Mastermind model and its affiliated products are trademarks.

Chapter 3: Foundations Of Time And Energy Management

1 J Cameron, *The Artist's Way: A spiritual path to higher creativity* (Souvenir Press, 2020)
2 Jabra, *Rebuilding Ourselves for the Hybrid Era* (2022), www.jabra.co.uk/hybridwork/2022, accessed 23 December 2022
3 C Yazeed, 'The dangers of courage culture and why Brené Brown isn't for Black folk', *Dr Carey Yazeed Blog*

(12 December 2021), https://drcareyyazeed.com/the-dangers-of-courage-culture-and-why-brene-brown-isnt-for-black-folk, accessed 23 December 2022

4 M Gandhi, *The Collected Works of Mahatma Gandhi*, Volume XII (The Publications Division, Ministry of Information and Broadcasting, Government of India, 1964)

5 N Eyal, *Indistractible: How to control your attention and choose your life* (Bloomsbury, 2019)

Chapter 4: Imposter Syndrome

1 R Fielding and C Chatterton, *Ten Minutes to Bed Little Unicorn* (Ladybird, 2020)

2 J Kastelic and T Ogilvie, 'Is the "impostor syndrome" affecting you and limiting your achievements?', *Canadian Veterinary Journal*, 63/4 (April 2022), 347–348, www.ncbi.nlm.nih.gov/pmc/articles/PMC8922383, accessed 18 April 2023

3 PR Clance and SA Imes, 'The imposter phenomenon in high achieving women: Dynamics and therapeutic intervention', *Psychotherapy: Theory, Research and Practice*, 15/3 (1978), 241–247, https://doi.org/10.1037/h0086006, accessed 5 May 2023

4 DM Bravata et al. 'Prevalence, predictors, and treatment of impostor syndrome: A systematic review', *Journal of General Internal Medicine*, 35 (2020), 1252–1275, http://dx.doi.org/10.1007/s11606-019-05364-1, accessed 5 May 2023

5 E Stoye, 'High levels of impostor syndrome found in female academics', *Chemistry World* (11 March 2019), www.chemistryworld.com/news/high-levels-of-impostor-syndrome-found-in-female-academics/3010214.article, accessed 27 March 2020

6 World Health Organization, 'Burn-out an "occupational phenomenon": International classification of diseases' (28 May 2019), www.who.int/news/item/28-05-2019-burn-out-an-occupational-phenomenon-international-classification-of-diseases, accessed 27 March 2020

7 K Glise, L Wiegner and I Jonsdottir, 'Long-term follow-up of residual symptoms in patients treated for stress-related exhaustion', *BMC Psychology*, 8/26 (2020), https://doi.org/10.1186/s40359-020-0395-8, accessed 5 May 2023

8   GOV.UK, 'Statutory Sick Pay (SSP): employer guide' (no date), www.gov.uk/employers-sick-pay/entitlement, accessed 17 April 2023

9   One of Many and its affiliated products are trademarks.

10 One Woman Conference: https://onewomanconference. co.uk, accessed 17 April 2023

11 OECD, *Education at a Glance 2022: OECD indicators* (OECD Publishing, 2022), https://doi.org/10.1787/3197152b-en, accessed 5 May 2023

12 M Obama, *Becoming* (Viking, 2018)

13 T Bhikkhu, trans, 'Sallatha Sutta: The arrow' (Access to Insight, BCBS Edition, 30 November 2013), www.accesstoinsight.org/tipitaka/sn/sn36/sn36.006.than.html, accessed 18 April 2023

14 H Stone and S Stone, *Embracing Ourselves: The voice dialogue manual* (Nataraj Publishing, New World Library, 1998)

15 Khan Academy, 'What is Newton's third law?' (no date), www.khanacademy.org/science/physics/forces-newtons-laws/newtons-laws-of-motion/a/what-is-newtons-third-law, accessed 18 April 2023

16 B Brown, 'The power of vulnerability', TED (2010), www.ted.com/talks/brene_brown_the_power_of_vulnerability, accessed 21 December 2022

17 H Stone and S Stone, *Embracing Ourselves*

18 S Chamine: www.positiveintelligence.com, accessed 18 April 2023

19 G Maté: https://compassionateinquiry.com, accessed 18 April 2023

20 R Schwartz: https://ifs-institute.com, accessed 18 April 2023

21 E Tolle and R Brand, 'Become awake now', *Under The Skin Podcast* (2020), https://youtu.be/6EwzvKF-o_Y, accessed 18 April 2023

22 T Shefali, *A Radical Awakening: Turn pain into power, embrace your truth, live free* (Yellow Kits, 2021)

23 J Fisher, *Healing the Fragmented Selves of Trauma Survivors: Overcoming internal self-alienation* (Taylor & Francis Ltd, 2017)

Chapter 5: Rebalancing To Wholeness Using The VOICE Framework

1   B Brown, 'The power of vulnerability', TED (2010), www.ted.com/talks/brene_brown_the_power_of_vulnerability, accessed 22 December 2022

2   B Brown, *Atlas of the Heart: Mapping meaningful connection and the language of human experience* (Vermilion, 2021)

3   Dalai Lama (@DalaiLama), 'You are human beings . . .' (27 July 2020), https://twitter.com/DalaiLama/status/1287683487454003201, accessed 18 February 2023

4   V Frankl, *Man's Search for Meaning: The classic tribute to hope from the Holocaust* (Rider, 2004)

5   L Eliot, 'Neurosexism: the myth that men and women have different brains', *Nature*, 566/7745 (2019), 453–454, www.researchgate.net/publication/331407425_Neurosexism_the_myth_that_men_and_women_have_different_brains, accessed 12 May 2023; G Rippon, *The Gendered Brain: The new neuroscience that shatters the myth of the female brain* (Random House, 2019)

6   A Saini, *Inferior: The true power of women and the science that shows it* (Harper Collins, 2018); C Fine, *Delusions of Gender: The real science behind sex differences* (WW Norton & Company, 2011)

7   L Brizendine, *The Female Brain* (Bantam, 2008)

8   B Katie, *Loving What Is: Four questions that can change your life* (Rider, 2002)

9   E Nagoski and A Nagoski, *Burnout: The secret to unlocking the stress cycle* (Ballantine Books, 2019)

10 A Mill et al. 'The role of co-occurring emotions and personality traits in anger expression', *Frontiers in Psychology*, 9/123 (2018), https://doi.org/10.3389/fpsyg.2018.00123, accessed 5 May 2023

11 T McCarthy, 'The edge of reason: The world's boldest climb and the man who conquered it', *The Guardian* (2017), www.theguardian.com/sport/2017/sep/10/climbing-el-capitan-alex-honnold-yosemite, accessed 18 April 2023

12 E Chai Vasarhelyi and J Chin, *Free Solo* (National Geographic Documentary Films, 2018)

13 ML Dixon and CS Dweck (2022), 'The amygdala and the prefrontal cortex: The co-construction of intelligent decision-making', *Psychological Review*, 129(6), 1414–1441, https://doi.org/10.1037/rev0000339, accessed 20 June 2023

14 A Grant, 'How free solo climber Alex Honnold faces fear', WorkLife with Adam Grant (20 September 2022), https://podcasts.apple.com/us/podcast/how-free-solo-climber-alex-honnold-faces-fear/id1346314086?i=1000580070495, accessed 21 September 2022

15 A Honnold, 'How I climbed a 3000 foot vertical cliff –
    without ropes', TED (2018), www.ted.com/talks/
    alex_honnold_how_i_climbed_a_3_000_foot_vertical_cliff_
    without_ropes, accessed 21 September 2022
16 P LaDouceur, 'What we fear more than death' (MentalHelp.
    net, 2013), www.mentalhelp.net/blogs/what-we-fear-
    more-than-death, accessed 21 September 2022
17 News.co.au, 'Here are Jerry Seinfeld's 10 funniest
    jokes', *New York Post* (17 April 2014), https://nypost.
    com/2014/04/17/here-are-jerry-seinfelds-10-funniest-
    jokes, accessed 21 September 2022

Chapter 6: Leadership Pathways

1 L Pritchett, M Woolcock and M Andrews, *Capability Traps?*
   The mechanisms of persistent implementation failure, Center for
   Global Development Working Paper, No. 234 (2010), http://
   dx.doi.org/10.2139/ssrn.1824519, accessed 5 May 2023
2 M Csikszentmihalyi, *Flow: The psychology of optimal*
   experience (Ingram International Inc, 2008)
3 R Hamilton, *Your Life, Your Legacy: An entrepreneur guide to*
   finding your flow (Achievers International, 2006)
4 'Service (n.1)', *Online Etymology Dictionary*, www.
   etymonline.com/word/service, accessed 18 April 2023
5 C Jung, *Psychological Types* (Routledge, 2022)
6 M Koerth and J Wolfe, 'Most personality quizzes are
   junk science: Take one that isn't' (FiveThirtyEight, 2019),
   https://projects.fivethirtyeight.com/personality-quiz,
   accessed 18 April 2023
7 Hogan Personality Inventory: www.hoganassessments.
   com/assessment/hogan-personality-inventory, accessed
   18 April 2023
8 R Dalio, 'Understand yourself. Understand others. Help
   others understand you' (Principles You, no date), https://
   principlesyou.com, accessed 18 April 2023
9 N Quenk, *Essentials of Myers-Briggs Type Indicator*
   Assessment (Wiley, 2009)
10 A Grant, 'Goodbye to MBTI, the fad that won't
   die', *Psychology Today* (18 September 2013), www.
   psychologytoday.com/gb/blog/give-and-take/201309/
   goodbye-mbti-the-fad-won-t-die, accessed 2 August 2022;

D Pittenger, 'Measuring the MBTI . . . and coming up short', *Journal of Career Planning and Employment*, 54 (1993), www.researchgate.net/publication/237675975_Measuring_the_MBTI_and_coming_up_short/link/585a82bb08ae3852d2571d2d/download, accessed 12 May 2023

11 Langley Group, 'Informal strengths assessment: Simple ways to realise strengths in people', https://langleygroup.com.au/informal-strengths-assessment-simple-ways-to-realise-strengths-in-people, accessed 15 August 2022

12 R Hamilton, 'Talent Dynamics', www.tdprofiletest.com/talent-dynamics-profiles, accessed 18 April 2023

Chapter 7: Career Pivots

1 Pivot (n.), Online Etymology Dictionary, www.etymonline.com/word/pivot, accessed 5 June 2023

2 M Schwantes, 'Steve Jobs said this was the most important tool he had ever encountered to make the most of his life', *Inc.* (13 December 2019), www.inc.com/marcel-schwantes/steve-jobs-said-this-is-most-important-tool-he-ever-encountered-to-make-most-of-his-life.html, accessed 6 June 2023

3 J Clear, '3-2-1: The process of life, joys of walking, and best hour of your week' (2 February 2023), https://jamesclear.com/3-2-1/february-2-2023, accessed 2 February 2023

4 S Jobs, 'Steve Jobs 2005 Stanford Commencement Address' (2008), www.youtube.com/watch?v=UF8uR6Z6KLc&t=50s, accessed 1 May 2022

5 J Campbell, *Pathways to Bliss: Mythology and personal transformation* (New World Library, 2004)

6 500 Women Scientists, 'Mission and vision' (no date), https://500womenscientists.org/mission-and-vision, accessed 12 May 2023

7 Department for Environment, Food & Rural Affairs, 'Carrier bag charges: retailers' responsibilities' (GOV.UK, 23 March 2015), www.gov.uk/guidance/carrier-bag-charges-retailers-responsibilities, accessed 23 December 2022

8 UK Public General Acts, 'Climate Change Act 2008', www.legislation.gov.uk/ukpga/2008/27/contents, accessed

9 October 2022; Acts of the Scottish Parliament, 'Climate Change (Scotland) Act 2009', www.legislation.gov.uk/asp/2009/12/contents, accessed 9 October 2022

9   Department for Environment, Food & Rural Affairs, 'Research and analysis – Single-use plastic carrier bags charge: data for England 2021 to 2022' (GOV.UK, 29 July 2022), www.gov.uk/government/publications/carrier-bag-charge-summary-of-data-in-england/single-use-plastic-carrier-bags-charge-data-for-england-2021-to-2022, accessed 9 October 2022

10   UK Parliament, 'Private Members' bills' (no date), www.parliament.uk/about/how/laws/bills/private-members, accessed 9 October 2022

11   R Lamb, *Environmental Levy on Plastic Bags (Scotland) Bill* (SPICe Briefing, 22 September 2005), https://archive2021.parliament.scot/SPICeResources/Research%20briefings%20and%20fact%20sheets/SB05-52.pdf, accessed 9 October 2022

12   NC Lutkehaus, *Margaret Mead: The making of an American icon* (Princeton University Press, 2008)

13   UK Parliament, '1897 foundation of the National Union of Women's Suffrage Society' (no date), www.parliament.uk/about/living-heritage/evolutionofparliament/2015-parliament-in-the-making/get-involved1/2015-banners-exhibition/alinah-azadeh/1897-founding-of-the-nuwss-gallery, accessed 20 February 2023

Chapter 8: Personal Branding

1   'Survey: business leaders start 2020 with lingering concerns about talent shortages and recession risk' (The Conference Board, 2 January 2020), www.conference-board.org/topics/c-suite-outlook/press/c-suite-survey-2020, accessed 20 February 2023

2   PwC, 'UK businesses set for radical change as almost a quarter admit their business model may not be viable in a decade – PwC's 26th Annual Global CEO Survey' (PwC Press Release, 16 January 2023), www.pwc.co.uk/press-room/press-releases/pwcs-26th-annual-global-ceo-survey.html, accessed 20 February 2023

3 P Cappelli, 'Your approach to hiring is all wrong', *Harvard Business Review* (May–June 2019), https://hbr. org/2019/05/your-approach-to-hiring-is-all-wrong, accessed 20 February 2023

4 Virgin (@Virgin), https://twitter.com/virgin, accessed 5 January 2023

5 R Branson (@richardbranson), https://twitter.com/ richardbranson, accessed 5 January 2023

6 A Vainer and A Zapesochini, '#IAmRemarkable', (Google, 2016), https://iamremarkable.withgoogle.com/, accessed 5 June 2023

7 L Cotter, 'LinkedIn content guide: How, what, why' (LinkedIn, 1 March 2021), www.linkedin.com/pulse/ linkedin-content-guide-how-what-why-lillian-cotter, accessed 19 December 2022

8 D Brosseau, *Ready to be a Thought Leader? How to increase your influence, impact, and success* (John Wiley & Sons, 2014)

Chapter 9: Professional Positioning

1 P Yang, 'How resume employment gaps affect interview changes of job applicants' (ResumeGo, no date), www. resumego.net/research/resume-employment-gaps, accessed 30 March 2022

2 J Hu, '99% of Fortune 500 companies use Applicant Tracking Systems' (Jobscan, 7 November 2019), www. jobscan.co/blog/99-percent-fortune-500-ats, accessed 30 March 2022

3 J Fuller et al. *Hidden Workers: Untapped talent* (Harvard Business School and Accenture, 2021), www.hbs.edu/ managing-the-future-of-work/Documents/research/ hiddenworkers09032021.pdf, accessed 12 May 2023

4 P Harris, '80% of resumes are rejected in less than 11 seconds . . .', Financial Post (8 September 2015), https:// financialpost.com/personal-finance/young-money/80- of-resumes-are-rejected-in-less-than-11-seconds-here- are-6-tips-on-surviving-that-brutal-first-cut, accessed 30 March 2022

5 Pregnant Then Screwed, 'Court of Appeal rule that the calculation of the Government's SEISS scheme discriminated against new mothers' (press release,

24 November 2021), https://pregnantthenscrewed.com/
press-release-court-of-appeal-rule-that-the-calculation-of-
the-governments-seiss-scheme-discriminated-against-new-
mothers, accessed 30 March 2022

6 P Yang, 'How resume employment gaps affect interview
chances of job applicants', (ResumeGo, no date), www.
resumego.net/research/resume-employment-gaps,
accessed 30 March 2022

7 P Yang, 'Settling the debate: one or two page resumes'
(ResumeGo, no date), www.resumego.net/research/one-
or-two-page-resumes, accessed 30 March 2022

8 'Unprofessional Email Addresses Can Hinder Job
Prospects' (HRReview, 14 Feb 2011), www.hrreview.co.uk/
hr-news/recruitment/unprofessional-email-addresses-can-
hinder-job-prospects/17426, accessed 5 June 2023

9 TS Mohr, 'Why women don't apply for jobs unless they're
100% qualified', *Harvard Business Review* (25 August 2014),
https://hbr.org/2014/08/why-women-dont-apply-for-
jobs-unless-theyre-100-qualified, accessed 30 March 2022

10 M Tomaszewski, 'Is a cover letter necessary in 2023? Do
I need a cover letter?' (ResumeLab, 12 August 2022),
https://resumelab.com/cover-letter/are-cover-letters-
necessary, accessed 30 March 2022

11 https://openai.com/blog/chatgpt

12 https://bard.google.com

13 www.microsoft.com/en-gb/bing

14 A Tunell, 'How to use ChatGPT to write your cover letter'
(Teal Career Hub, 19 January 2023), www.tealhq.com/
post/how-to-use-chatgpt-to-write-your-cover-letter,
accessed 20 February 2023

15 R Pelta and J Skowronski, 'We asked ChatGPT to write
resumes and cover letters. Here's what it got right and
wrong' (Forage, 16 December 2022), www.theforage.com/
blog/news/chatgpt-cover-letter, accessed 20 February 2023

16 A Fennel, 'Job interview statistics' (StandOutCV,
December 2022), https://standout-cv.com/job-interview-
statistics, accessed 21 December 2022

17 Indeed Editorial Team, 'How to use the STAR interview
technique in interviews' (Indeed, 14 December 2020),
https://uk.indeed.com/career-advice/interviewing/star-
technique, accessed 12 January 2021

18 J Schifeling, '9 steps to solving an impossible brain teaser
in a tech interview (without breaking a sweat)', *The Muse*

(19 June 2020), www.themuse.com/advice/9-steps-to-solving-an-impossible-brain-teaser-in-a-tech-interview-without-breaking-a-sweat, accessed 12 February 2021

19 Glassdoor, 'Software engineer interview question' (no date), www.glassdoor.co.uk/Interview/You-have-a-100-coins-laying-flat-on-a-table-each-with-a-head-side-and-a-tail-side-10-of-them-are-heads-up-90-are-tails-QTN_290837.htm, accessed 12 February 2021

20 J Nestor, *Breath: The new science of a lost art* (Penguin Life, 2021)

Chapter 10: Propelling Strategies

1 World Economic Forum, *Global Gender Gap Report 2022* (13 July 2022), www.weforum.org/reports/global-gender-gap-report-2022/digest, accessed 14 August 2022

2 Office for National Statistics, 'Gender pay gap in the UK: 2022' (Office for National Statistics statistical bulletin, 26 October 2022), www.ons.gov.uk/employmentandlabourmarket/peopleinwork/earningsandworkinghours/bulletins/genderpaygapintheuk/2022, accessed 14 November 2022

3 D Campbell, 'Record numbers of women reach 30 child-free in England and Wales', *The Guardian* (27 January 2022), www.theguardian.com/lifeandstyle/2022/jan/27/women-child-free-30-ons, accessed 14 November 2022

4 T Shadwell, 'The second mortgage: How Britain's soaring childcare costs leave parents unable to afford to work' (itvNews Insight, 27 October 2022), www.itv.com/news/2022-10-26/the-second-mortgage-how-childcare-costs-leave-parents-unable-to-afford-to-work, accessed 14 November 2022

5 Fawcett Society, 'Mothers on the lowest incomes are eight times more at risk of losing their job due to school closures in the UK' (8 January 2021), www.fawcettsociety.org.uk/news/mothers-on-the-lowest-incomes-eight-times-more-at-risk-of-losing-their-job-due-to-school-closures-in-the-uk, accessed 20 December 2022

6 Pregnant Then Screwed, 'The gender pay gap – do women deserve to be paid less because they have a uterus?' (no date), https://pregnantthenscrewed.com/gender-pay-gap-women-deserve-paid-less-uterus, accessed 20 December 2022

7 N Omoigui, 'Salary transparency in job ads reaches six year low', HR Magazine (2 November 2022), www.hrmagazine. co.uk/content/news/salary-transparency-in-job-ads-reaches-six-year-low, accessed 20 December 2022

8 Glassdoor, 'Glassdoor study reveals what job seekers are looking for', Glassdoor blog (25 July 2018), www.glassdoor. com/employers/blog/salary-benefits-survey, accessed 20 December 2022

9 M Johanson, 'Why companies don't post salaries in job adverts' (BBC Worklife, 22 September 2021), www.bbc. com/worklife/article/20210921-why-companies-dont-post-salaries-in-job-adverts, accessed 12 May 2023

10 A Omeokwe, 'Study finds salary-history bans boost pay for African-Americans, women', *The Wall Street Journal* (18 June 2020), www.wsj.com/articles/study-finds-salary-history-bans-boost-pay-for-african-americans-women-11592472602, accessed 20 December 2022

11 A Grant (@AdamMGrant), 'Hey managers: don't ask people what they earned in their last job' (2 July 2020), https://twitter.com/AdamMGrant/status/1278681022473830400, accessed 10 July 2023

12 www.glassdoor.co.uk/index.htm

13 https://uk.indeed.com

14 https://uk.linkedin.com

15 www.monster.co.uk

16 www.checkasalary.co.uk

17 Technologist Confidant, 'Salary negotiations in the UK' (Technologist Confidant: Career Advice, 10 June 2022), www.technologistconfidant.com/post/salary-negotiations-in-the-uk, accessed 23 December 2022

18 Randstad, 'Negotiating your benefits package beyond the salary' (19 December 2022), www.randstad.co.uk/career-advice/salary/negotiating-your-benefits-package-beyond-salary, accessed 30 November 2022

19 L Babcock and S Laschever, *Women Don't Ask: The high cost of avoiding negotiation and positive strategies for change* (Bantam, 2007)

20 C Ubiera, 'Out of luck: You're 250 times more likely to be hit by lightning and 80 times more likely to be attacked by a shark than win the lotto', The US Sun (11 February 2022), www.the-sun.com/money/4663302/lottery-winning-odds-statistics-money, accessed 30 November 2022

21 R Gillham, 'Women salary negotiation (10 tips for
    2022)', Blinkist (24 September 2022), www.blinkist.com/
    magazine/posts/women-salary-negotiation-tips, accessed
    30 November 2022; M Clark, 'International Women's
    Day: A guide to negotiating a higher salary', *Independent*
    (8 March 2022), www.independent.co.uk/life-style/
    salary-negotiate-raise-pay-gap-b2031523.html, accessed
    30 November 2022
22 I Hankel, 'What is a 30-60-90-day plan and how to amaze
    interviewers by presenting one' (Cheeky Scientist, no date),
    https://cheekyscientist.com/what-is-a-30-60-90-day-
    plan-and-how-to-amaze-interviewers-by-presenting-one,
    accessed 30 November 2022
23 A Deutschman, *Change or Die: The three keys to change at
    work and in life* (Harper Business, 2008)
24 T Goetz, 'How Facebook uses feedback loops: meet Rypple'
    (Wired, 20 June 2011), www.wired.com/2011/06/facebook-
    uses-feedback-loops, accessed 5 January 2021

Chapter 11: Making It Happen

1 J Martin, 'Lead the Change', presentation at One of Many,
   Stratford Manor (9 October 2022)
2 ERC, '3 ways to calculate your training and development
   budget', *myERC blog* (18 October 2018), www.yourerc.
   com/blog/post/3-ways-to-calculate-a-training-and-
   development-budget-for-your-organization, accessed
   23 December 2022
3 C Gallo, 'The one investment Warren Buffet says will
   change your life (and it's not a stock)', *Forbes* (30 November
   2017), www.forbes.com/sites/carminegallo/2017/11/30/
   the-one-investment-warren-buffet-says-will-change-your-
   life-and-its-not-a-stock/, accessed 5 June 2023
4 K Satyarthi and M Yousafzai, The Nobel Peace Prize, 2014,
   www.nobelprize.org/prizes/peace/2014/yousafzai/facts,
   accessed 18 April 2023
5 M Obama, The White House, www.whitehouse.gov/about-
   the-white-house/first-families/michelle-obama, accessed
   18 April 2023
6 B Doherty, 'The key moments of Jacinda Arden's time
   as prime minister', *The Guardian* (19 January 2023),

www.theguardian.com/world/2023/jan/19/the-key-moments-of-jacinda-ardern-time-as-prime-minister-of-nz-new-zealand, accessed 18 April 2023

7 G Thunberg, United Nations, UN Web TV, General Assembly, 2019, https://media.un.org/en/asset/k1p/k1p8j4fqy0, accessed 18 April 2023

Conclusion

1 M Angelou, *I Know Why the Caged Bird Sings* (Virago, 1984)

Acknowledgements

It is an absolute privilege to do this work. I do not do it alone; I'm supported by many wonderful people. I'd especially like to thank my husband, Mark, for the gifts you have brought into my life: our children Oscar, Jenson and Elsie. For me to travel and deliver training in person, both Mark and my parents have supported me with the practical logistics, as well as words of encouragement. On that note, thank you to my mum, Chris, and my dad, John, for moving to Bollington to bring our family even closer together.

A special acknowledgement to my best friend, Katie, for your unconditional love and for showing me the full range of emotional dexterity. To my oldest friends, Catrina, Lauren and Carolyn, for always being my champions, ready to relax, hold an intervention or create mischief, depending on what's required.

The Bolly Mums, it really does take a village to raise a child and you are always there at a moment's notice.

To my team, Lexi, Kath, Sanja, Laura and Sam, for doing things better than I could ever do them myself. My amazing mentors, Helen, Jo, Annie, Susie, Lisa and Daniel, you are all an inspiration to me, and I have benefitted from your wisdom time and again. To Sharon for being my buddy on the road to becoming an International Coaching Federation Professional Certified Coach and welcoming my most pointed questions. I can't wait to continue the journey to Master Certified Coach. I would also like to thank the entire One of Many, Dent, Voice Dialogue and Catalyst communities for your accountability, insights and support.

Beta readers, you know who you are, and this book is so much clearer for your thoughts. To Susanna for bringing your expertise as a specialist in psychological trauma. To Sadia for your DEI knowledge, ensuring this manuscript is accessible for all. Rachel, you are a superstar, thank you for using your natural talent for accuracy and fact-checking my references and data. To Felicity (Fliss) for going through the manuscript line by line and making sure I used the most impactful phrasing.

I would especially like to thank the team at Rethink Press for all their hard work and support. In particular, Kathy and Anke, for meticulously shaping the manuscript and book design so beautifully. Sophie, for her support with the launch, and founders Lucy and Joe, for their invaluable expertise, particularly during the early stages of writing.

Finally, I'd like to thank my clients for trusting me to help them feel happy and fulfilled by moving towards wholeness. You are all my biggest teachers, and it makes me incredibly excited to know you are out in the world, doing things differently and creating a ripple effect. Many of the ideas in this book have come about from joining the dots between the themes of our coaching conversations. The stories in this book were only made possible by the courage of my clients who shared their innermost fears to serve a bigger purpose. I thank you wholeheartedly for your contributions.

The Author

 As the founder of Intentional Careers and host of a top ten UK podcast Women in STEM Career and Confidence, Dr Hannah Roberts is an award-winning coach on a mission to eradicate inequality in the workplace by guiding women to design careers for fulfilment, with a mindset for leadership, to build progressive workplace cultures where every individual feels valued.

Hannah is uniquely positioned as a scientist and mum of three with a background in the corporate world and academia. She was managing director of a spin-out company before pivoting into coaching, speaking and training in 2019. She has clients spanning six continents and is a certified One of Many Women's Leadership Coach and Trainer, with the Professional Certified Coach credential from the International Coaching Federation and has been a member of the Forbes Coaches Council since 2022.

Hannah gives keynote speeches and workshops at industry and academic conferences and events globally, including, Microsoft, HSBC, GSK, AstraZeneca, Optica, EDF, Magnox, Oxford University Press, Waters, and over twenty-six UK universities. In particular, she is active with the women's and leadership networks within these organisations. Over the years she has been featured in *Forbes, Chemistry World, Nature Careers* and other major publications.

When she is not coaching, speaking or training, Hannah is at home with her family in Bollington, UK, enjoying nature as a playground on her doorstep and swimming both indoors with Satellites Masters Squad and outdoors in rivers, lakes and the sea.

Hannah believes when you value yourself, you are valued by others and you'll make a valuable contribution to the world. For more information visit **https:// hannahnikeroberts.com**.

To find out more about hiring Hannah as a speaker or for all media enquiries please visit **https:// hannahnikeroberts.com/contact**.

🌐 https://hannahnikeroberts.com

in www.linkedin.com/in/hannahrobertscoaching

f www.facebook.com/drhannahroberts

🐦 @HannahNikeR

📷 @drhannahroberts

Printed in Great Britain
by Amazon

27751434R00153